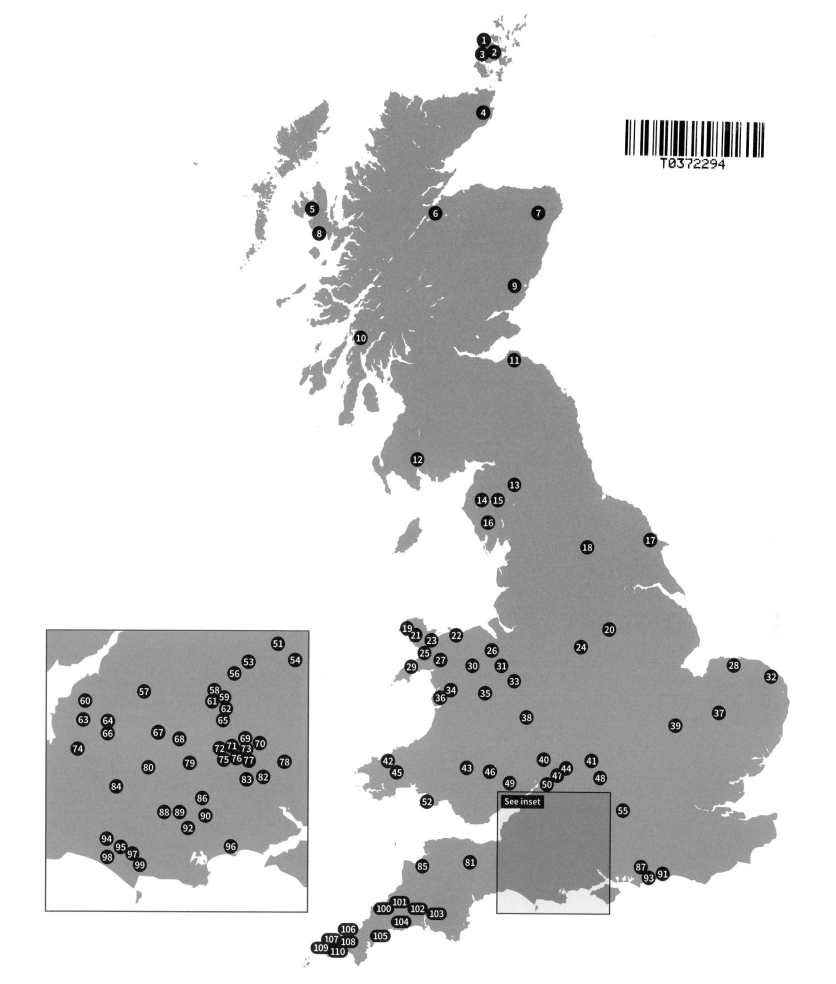

T0372294

Aerial Atlas
of Ancient Britain

Aerial Atlas
of Ancient Britain

David R. Abram   Foreword by Alice Roberts

Frontispiece: Badbury Rings, Dorset

First published in the United Kingdom in 2022 by
Thames & Hudson Ltd, 181A High Holborn, London WC1V 7QX

First published in the United States of America in 2022 by
Thames & Hudson Inc., 500 Fifth Avenue, New York, New York 10110

Reprinted 2024

Aerial Atlas of Ancient Britain © 2022 Thames & Hudson Ltd, London

Text © 2022 David R. Abram

Foreword © 2022 Alice Roberts

Photographs © David R. Abram, except those listed on p. 269

Designed by Maggi Smith

British Library Cataloguing-in-Publication Data
A catalogue record for this book is available from the British Library

Library of Congress Control Number 2022931891

ISBN 978-0-500-02416-4

Printed and bound in China by C&C Offset Printing Co. Ltd

MIX
Paper | Supporting
responsible forestry
FSC® C008047

Be the first to know about our new releases,
exclusive content and author events by visiting
thamesandhudson.com
thamesandhudsonusa.com
thamesandhudson.com.au

Contents

Foreword

I love walking. The physicality of that connection with a landscape, the opening of a view as you crest a hill or turn a headland, the different textures underfoot and on the retina, the sun, wind and rain. The sighting of a sea eagle over a loch, a seal near the coast, a clump of snowdrops in early February – these all feel like natural gifts, blessings. But on most walks I am also keenly aware of a human presence, even in some of the wildest, emptiest places. I might be far away from modern conurbations, roads or even fields, but still there are traces of people. People who are no longer with us. It feels as though the countryside is full of their ghosts. I don't believe in any sort of life after death; as a humanist, I accept the finite nature of life. And yet, those traces persist, hundreds, even thousands of years after their creators are not just dead but forgotten. In a very real way, the ancestors are still with us, all around in the landscape.

I seek out those traces on walks: gravitating towards hill forts, tumuli and barrows. I place them in the landscape, map their presence in my mind, discovering constellations of monuments that form a nexus across place and time. Gravity holds me down among mud and grass and stone, but in my mind's eye I can hover like a kestrel above the landscape and see the patterns written on it by the ancients.

That view from the air lets us understand those patterns in a different way. It is the answer to the question: why is it here? It helps us approach the original meaning of those monuments – whilst suggesting new meanings and relevance for us in the present.

David Abram has captured the landscape of the past, walking in the British landscape but sending his vision high to glimpse astonishingly beautiful views, bathed in early morning or late evening sunlight. Long, dark shadows define and outline, reminding us of the passage of time. His pilgrimages to ancient places fill the pages of this book, taking us on an aerial, visual journey from the depths of the Ice Age and the distant, fleeting traces of a Palaeolithic presence, through the arrival of the first farmers, the first metalworkers, and on to the end of the Iron Age.

The views may have changed since the monuments were created; Britain would have been a much icier, less wooded and then more forested place at various times in the past. Paviland Cave is now on the coast of the Gower Peninsula in South Wales, but when a young man was buried there more than 30,000 years ago, it was 110 kilometers (70 miles) from the sea. The Severn Estuary would have been a wide, grassy plain with the palaeo-Severn snaking across it. The sea level was 100 metres (330 feet) lower than today, with so much water locked up in ice sheets, and yet the outcrop of rock we see today would have been familiar to those hunter-gatherers. The Neolithic farmers who created the cairns at Rubha an Dùnain on the Isle of Skye, and the later Vikings who built their harbour there, cannot have failed to appreciate the stunning setting. David's quest to document the traces of prehistoric ancestors in the landscape has seen him take his cameras far and wide. You will find sites here that you haven't been to or perhaps heard of (and if you're anything like me, you'll start planning an itinerary to take them in), but you will also find familiar sites – and see them with new eyes: Stonehenge in snow, Silbury Hill like a shield boss, the deep furrows of Maiden Castle.

From an elevated viewpoint, we see these places in context. And we see generations of people returning to old haunts, the traces of more recent ancestors laid on top of or alongside the ancient monuments, possessing their power: the ruins of a Norman cathedral within the Iron Age ramparts of Old Sarum, the Roman road piercing through one of the Priddy rings, the hedgerows that respect earlier boundaries, the turns of the plough around a long barrow.

The beauty of these images invites you in, to see the ancient monuments of Britain from a new perspective. We're just the latest people in this place.

Alice Roberts

Feorlig Cairns, Loch Caroy, Isle of Skye

Introduction

Compiled over several years of travel, research and writing, this collection of photographs represents the fruit of three parallel journeys. The first was physical, involving countless hours of driving, cycling and walking to archaeological sites across the British Isles. The second was a quest to find out as much as I could about the monuments and the eras in which they originated. And the third was wrestling the many thousands of images and pages of notes I gathered along the way into the form you have in front of you now.

One of the great joys of the endeavour was that it enabled me to experience Britain's diverse landscapes at their most alluring: when they were gilded by dawn light, dusted in snow and basking under blue skies. Moreover, as many of the shoots were carried out during the Covid pandemic, the roads were frequently empty and locations deserted – a privilege seldom enjoyed these days.

No less satisfying, in a different way, was the research I carried out on the sites themselves. Much more is known about them than I had anticipated, though the telling details I needed were often buried deep in obscure archaeological monographs. Sifting through the data tables, graphs and academic prose felt at times like searching for pretty pebbles on a vast shingle beach. But sooner or later, the revealing detail I sought – a description of an extraordinary object unearthed during a dig or a feature hidden deep beneath the soil – would come to light, inspiring, perhaps, a follow-up visit to a museum I'd never been to, or a search for an out-of-print book penned by the eighteenth-century antiquarian who had first excavated the monument.

When deciding how best to present the material, I have allowed myself to be guided by my own relative ignorance. Despite being fascinated by prehistory since childhood, I had only the vaguest grasp when I began work on this project of what defined the various epochs and how one morphed into another. I knew, for example, that the Great Henge at Avebury dated from the Neolithic era, but not how it related to the earthworks on nearby Windmill Hill. If you had asked me when the Bronze Age began, or when people started riding horses on these islands or building hillforts, I would have struggled.

I did, however, wish to find out the ways in which human society in Britain changed from the end of the Ice Age until the arrival of the Romans, and how the many monuments I had visited exemplified this story. Approaching a subject in this way, as a non-specialist, has one distinct advantage: you develop a very clear sense of what a reader needs to know.

However, formulating a chronological narrative to contextualize the sites proved a challenge. Archaeologists tend to shy away from what might be described as 'the bigger picture'. There are good reasons for this – principally the risk of opening oneself up to criticism from one's peers of 'over-simplification'. But with no academic reputation at risk, I felt free to dive right into these choppy pedagogic waters and, while the rest of the country baked sourdough loaves through the spring of 2020, I spent months devouring piles of archaeology books and articles, and condensing great sweeps of prehistory into a few pages of writing (which, I should add, were checked very thoroughly by a team of expert reviewers before going to print; see 'Acknowledgments' on p. 269).

The result, I hope, is the book I had always wanted to read myself – one that treads an acceptable line between platitudinous generality and overwhelming detail, but manages, at the same time, to convey a sense of the richness and diversity of our prehistoric heritage.

Old Ways and Places

A less tangible consequence of these three interwoven journeys was the way they formulated a new mental map of Britain – one dominated to a large extent by the country's natural landscapes.

Living in the modern era, our sense of place and space tends to be disrupted by motorways, train lines and cities. But in the distant past, when rivers were the principal travel arteries, and sacred sites rather than settlements were where people gathered in large numbers, landscape and topography mattered a lot more. Types of rock and their respective uses, for example, would have been common knowledge in the Neolithic, as would the land and maritime routes connecting the great henges and other ceremonial centres to which communities must have travelled at auspicious times of year to worship, trade and socialize. Later, these same sites took on added significance, attracting migrants from the Low Countries who brought with them knowledge of metal-making and left in their wake the burial mounds that still blister the chalk uplands of Wessex.

Exploring prehistory lets us rediscover these forgotten horizons, developing in the process a keener sense of which places were important in the distant past and how they were interconnected. Similarities between stone circles or types of tomb join regions as disparate as North Wales and Orkney, or the Cotswolds and Cumbria. Stone axes polished smooth more than five thousand years ago hold a different significance after you have climbed to the rock outcrop where they were originally quarried.

Such experiences guide us into the mindset of our distant forebears, revealing, if we're lucky, what they valued and venerated, and why. They also hold the potential to subtly transform the way we perceive these islands.

The Neolithic henge at Mayburgh in Cumbria (see p. 98) is a prime example. Despite the stream of motorway traffic roaring past nowadays, this wonderful site is little known beyond the region where it stands. Yet judging by its impressive size, and the extraordinary amount of work that went into creating it, the monument must have been of huge significance in its day. Comprising hundreds of thousands of river pebbles, the circle sits next to what would have been the principal north–south route between the Lake District and the Pennines (as it still does, of course). People across Britain would have known it by name; many must have travelled here at some point in their lifetime. So these days, on my journeys to and from Scotland, I always make a point of stopping at Mayburgh, the navel of ancient Britain, walking three times around the henge and touching the stately monolith at its centre for good luck before continuing onwards. By doing so, I feel more deeply connected not only to the landscape of the Eden Valley, but also to the people who inhabited it thousands of years ago.

It is my hope that this book will reveal such discoveries, inspiring people to seek out the lost geographies of our ancestors. Fundamentally, we inhabit the same ground they did. It may have changed almost beyond recognition in some instances, but the effect on our state of mind of a wide-ranging view or prominent river confluence is essentially the same now as it was then, forging an experiential link between us and the people who came before. Such places are everywhere when you learn to see them.

The Aerial Perspective

An elevated viewpoint is a powerful way to explore prehistoric sites and landscapes. What may appear as clusters of random lumps, bumps and banks at ground level often resolve into striking forms when viewed from the air. Neolithic long barrows take on a protective, benevolent feel with the valley below (instead of the sky above) as their backdrop. Alignments and reciprocities between structures and landforms – such as the pivotal position of a stone circle amid an amphitheatre of hills, or a Bronze Age burial site at the head of a combe – are also revealed to dramatic effect from the height of a hovering kestrel.

Sceptics may dismiss such connections, claiming they cannot be proven or that they are unlikely to have existed at all if invisible from the ground. But looking at the photographs in this book, it is hard not to agree that many prehistoric monuments were a form of landscape art, created in relation to the ridges, rivers and horizons around them.

A hilltop that appears to be aligned on an axis with a tomb may not be visible from the monument itself, but that connection may still exist. Our ancestors would have known the precise position of that hill (even when it may have been obscured by trees), and would probably have related it to the point where the sun or moon rose and set on auspicious days in the calendar.

Over the years, as I have developed a better understanding of ceremonial landscapes in prehistory, I have tended to seek out these connections and use them to anchor my compositions. How significant they may have been is something I prefer to leave to the viewer (I am a photographer not an archaeologist after all) but I hope such resonances provoke interest as well as being pleasing to look at.

How to Use this Book

The locations are arranged in roughly chronological order, beginning with early hominin sites of the deep Palaeolithic and ending just prior to the Roman invasion. They are divided up according to the 'Three Age System' – originally proposed by the Danish museum curator C. J. Thomsen – which defines epochs according to their predominant technologies (stone, bronze or iron).

As a conceptual framework, this approach has its disadvantages, imposing distinctions that would not have been recognizable to people who lived in these different eras. But it nevertheless serves a useful purpose. While researching, I found it enormously helpful to be able to pinpoint the differences between the eras in such things as tools, ritual practices, trade, settlement and land use.

This essential chronology is set out in the introductions that precede each of the four main sections. As well as being something you can dip in and out of, the book was written to be read from start to finish: by reading the introductions before the texts accompanying the sites, you should gain a more vivid sense of how individual monuments relate to their eras and the extent to which they mirror the changes taking place at the time they were in use.

Britain holds tens of thousands of prehistoric sites, from which we have selected some of the most spectacular and significant. Collectively, they illustrate how ways of life developed over long periods of time: how the hunter-gather communities of the Palaeolithic and Mesolithic gave way to the first herder-farmers from northern France, who crossed the English Channel around the start of the fourth millennium bringing with them pots of seed grain and domesticated sheep, pigs and calves, to pioneer a radically new way of relating to the British landscape; how their descendants built great earth circles from the chalk soils of Wessex, erecting stone-lined tombs and, several centuries on, the colossal enclosures of megaliths that, midway through the third millennium BC, attracted the attention of other incomers from northern Europe, who, in turn, brought with them knowledge of metalworking, and new beliefs and customs.

The story of how these migrants displaced the builders of Stonehenge and Avebury is traced across the British landscape to this day, along with the outlines of the field enclosures, farmsteads and hillforts erected by subsequent generations, when the 'bow wave' of Roman influence began to be felt.

These wonders are hidden in plain sight all around us. Discovering them through the following pages will guide you to some wonderful places that, quite apart from providing insights into the past, may fundamentally alter the way you think and feel about the land beneath your feet. If I have learned one thing after my prehistoric odyssey around these islands, it is that we should trust our ancestors: they knew all the best places.

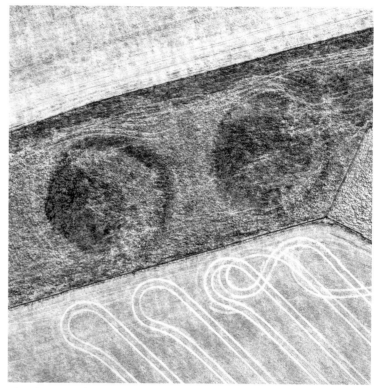

Winterbourne Stoke, Wiltshire

The Palaeolithic and Mesolithic

For the duration of the Ice Age (aka 'the Pleistocene'), which lasted from roughly 2.5 million to 12,000 years ago, Britain was either a peninsula or a remote island off the far northwestern fringe of Europe. Its climate, like that of the Continent, was determined by the ebb and flow of giant ice fields, which periodically subsumed most of the land mass. These cold periods occurred in cycles of between 41,000 and 100,000 years, determined by subtle shifts in the earth's axis and orbit, and were interrupted by warm interludes when temperatures were comparable to, or slightly higher than, those of the present day.

The results were dramatic changes in both weather and landscape: regions of Britain that were at one time subtropical, supporting populations of hippos, elephants and lions, could in a matter of decades be plunged into Arctic conditions, where the deciduous forests and marshland were replaced by wind-blown tundra roamed by woolly mammoths, rhinos, hyenas and wolves.

Measuring Time

Establishing a chronology for these climatic oscillations has been possible through analysis of sediment extracted from the seabed. Core samples hold myriads of shell particles containing oxygen of two different atomic weights, whose relative values alter according to whether they were formed in warm or cold periods.

Once the isotopic values manifest in these core samples had been calculated and listed on a scale, a benchmark was needed to fix an absolute date against which they could be calibrated. This came when a correlation was found between entries on the isotope chart with a reversal in the earth's magnetic field observed by geologists in rock dated to 736,000 years ago. The date provided a baseline by which everything after it could be reliably fixed.

This chronology could also be cross-referenced with cores drilled out of the Greenland ice cap, the deepest parts of which (3,000 metres [10,000 feet] below ground level) were laid down hundreds of thousands of years ago. Each summer, surface ice in the Arctic melts and acquires a layer of dust particles. When these re-freeze, they show up as dark bands in the core samples – the Arctic equivalent of tree rings. These mirror the isotopic fluctuations apparent in seabed sediment and could therefore be used to corroborate the latter.

Stone Tools

With the exception of a few rare fossilized bones, the only objects to have survived from the time of early hominins and the first anatomically modern humans in Britain are the stone tools they left behind. By scrutinizing these, along with the soil layers in which they were found, archaeologists have been able to deduce a surprising amount about life in these distant epochs.

The way the tools evolved over time sheds light on the kind of food people ate, how they obtained and prepared it, how far they roamed across the landscape and even the extent of their cognitive abilities. The animal bones, pollen grains and snail shells detectable in the same layers can also yield information about the plants that grew at the time the tools were deposited, and thus what the climate was like.

A complex taxonomy has been established for categorizing the various hand axes, scrapers, blades and other lithic residues that have come to light at sites across Europe. Named after the locations where they were first discovered, these 'toolkits' are often associated with groups of mammalian remains to define a particular cultural phase, which can in most cases be correlated with specific climatic periods.

To the uninitiated, the labels – whether 'Mousterian', 'Acheulian', 'Aurignacian', 'Gravettian' or 'Creswellian' – can be difficult to keep track of, which is why we have largely avoided using them in this book (along with the multitude of monikers for different warm and cold phases). Instead, the vast spans of time and artefacts associated with them will, in the following pages, be discussed in the context of specific sites, citing date ranges where these are available. Readers wishing to delve more deeply into the extraordinary work carried out by the palaeontologists and archaeologists who have shed light on the mysteries of these remarkable locations will find suggestions in the Further Reading section on p. 268.

The Lower Palaeolithic

Rudimentary flint tools uncovered by cliff erosion on the east coast indicate that the first hominins to colonize Britain were probably a species known as *Homo antecessor*, who arrived in the centuries before 500,000 BC, bringing with them the first hand axes in their toolkits. One site in particular, Happisburgh in Norfolk (see p. 17), has yielded a wealth of material relating to this period in the Lower Palaeolithic.

Half a million years ago, a warm interlude in the Ice Age enabled a second species of early hominin called *Homo heidelbergensis* to settle on what is now the south coast of England, where the first evidence of hunting and butchering has been identified at Boxgrove near Chichester (see p. 18).

The Middle and Upper Palaeolithic

Britain was populated only intermittently in the next warm spell, which lasted from 424,000 until 374,000 years ago and appears to have been completely devoid of hominins between 180,000 and 60,000 years ago. At this point, groups of Neanderthals began to migrate into the region, following herds of mammoth and reindeer, which they processed using skilfully made bifacial hand axes.

The first anatomically modern humans to enter Britain arrived between 35,000 and 30,000 years ago. This is the period represented by the remains discovered at Goat's Hole Cave near Paviland on the Gower Peninsula (see p. 21). Sea levels were considerably lower at this point, enabling mammoth hunters to press northwards from what are now France and the Low Countries into the belt of Siberian-style tundra that enveloped most of the land mass. It is likely such visits were only occasional, made during relatively short phases of warm weather.

By 16,000 BC, Britain was once again in the grip of a protracted cold period, dubbed the 'Last Glacial Maximum', in which ice sheets 3 kilometres (nearly 2 miles) deep cloaked parts of what is now Scotland, with lobes stretching as far south as modern-day Glamorgan and Norfolk.

The Windermere Interstadial

Of the spells of warmer weather that punctuated the final phase of the Ice Age in Britain, the most important from the point of view of human occupation is one, known as the 'Windermere Interstadial', that started, quite abruptly, 12,700 years ago. Within just a few years of the climatic turnaround, hunter-gatherers were following herds of wild horses and red deer deep into the British peninsula, establishing seasonal camps, and eventually more permanent bases, in caves along the south coast of Devon, in the Mendip Hills and the Peak District.

This period of the Upper Palaeolithic saw a dramatic evolution in material culture. Stone tools became more sophisticated and new types of weapons, including flint blades bound with twine and resin on to wooden shafts, and spears hurled using throwers, enabled people to hunt a wider range of animals across a broader spectrum of habitats. Personal adornment, ceremonial burials and art (wall paintings, etchings and portable pieces of sculpture) also emerged before a sudden return to cold conditions forced populations back south.

Doggerland

From the middle of the Upper Palaeolithic period until melting ice caused sea levels to rise around the eighth millennium BC, an area of ecologically rich land roughly the size of the Netherlands joined the British peninsula to the Continent. Known today as 'Doggerland', this now-submerged landscape was probably among the most densely populated parts of Europe thanks to its diversity of habitats and fauna.

That people lived and hunted in the region 13,000–12,000 years ago, when sea levels were 120 metres (400 feet) lower than today, we know from objects – including antler harpoons and flint tools – retrieved by fishing trawlers and washed up on beaches on either side of the southern North Sea.

Seismic data gleaned from oil and gas surveys have enabled geologists to reconstruct this lost prehistoric topography, which comprised bands of low hills separated by wooded valleys, expanses of marshland, lagoons and gravel beaches – an optimal environment for hunter-gatherers.

It was via Doggerland that the people who migrated to Britain throughout the Palaeolithic period first arrived, and by means of which Mesolithic pioneers crossed from Scandinavia to Yorkshire and other points along the east coast. Around 6200 BC, however, after melting ice in the Arctic prompted a rise in sea levels, the region become gradually inundated, forcing people on to higher ground further west and east.

The Mesolithic

A last gasp of the Ice Age brought the Windermere Interstadial warm spell to an end roughly 12,000 years ago, once again displacing populations to more habitable parts of Europe. But the cold snap lasted only a few centuries. By 8800 BC, groups of hunter-gatherers were once again returning through Doggerland to Britain, heralding the start of what archaeologists term the 'Mesolithic' era.

In many respects, there was little to differentiate the material culture of this time from the latter phases of the Upper Palaeolithic. People still lived a largely nomadic, hunter-gatherer existence, moving between seasonal camps. But as the climate grew warmer, the herds of wild horses that had previously sustained them were either hunted out or moved to cooler climes, to be replaced by species better adapted to the mixed woodland of pine, birch and alder that replaced the tundra.

To hunt elk, aurochs, deer and wild boar, a greater range of tools and hunting techniques were deployed. Ever more slender shards of flint, known as 'microliths' by archaeologists, were used to make

Cheddar Gorge, Mendip Hills, Somerset

arrowheads, harpoons and spear tips. Over time, tanged or barbed blades emerged and, when fired from newly invented bows, these proved more effective for bringing down animals, which must have both led to an increase in population and contributed to some extent to the demise of the species on which human life depended.

Gradually, Mesolithic people spread westwards, beyond the chalklands of Wessex and into Wales, and north to the furthest corners of Scotland. Some created wooden structures for shelter, as at Star Carr in Yorkshire (see p. 24) and Blick Mead in Wiltshire, sites to which they seem to have returned over many years. At Stonehenge, a cluster of post holes was erected close to the spot where the great stone circle would be raised thousands of years later, hinting at the existence of some kind of ceremonial monument based on observation of solar or lunar cycles.

The Mesolithic in Britain, however, was to prove less resilient in the face of competition from Neolithic pioneers than it did in other parts of northern Europe. Within just a few centuries, the exclusively hunter-gatherer way of life had all but disappeared from these shores, superseded by one that supplemented hunting with cereal cultivation and livestock herding.

Happisburgh Norfolk

Happisburgh (pronounced 'Haze-borough'), on the northeast coast of Norfolk, is best known for its strident red-and-white lighthouse, whose nocturnal blinking has warded off passing ships since 1790. But this windblown little village on the edge of England has a far more astounding claim to fame.

In 2010 a team of palaeontologists rummaging around the base of its sandy cliffs discovered fragments of flint tools and cut-marked bones. Flushed out by high spring tides, they had been embedded in a layer of grey sedimentary rock known to geologists as the 'Cromer Forest-bed Formation' – the remains of ancient mud flats lining what we now know as the River Thames, which around 450,000 years ago were bulldozed southwards to its present course by massive glaciers.

From their context and appearance, the tools were dated to around 866,000 years ago, making them by far the oldest traces of humans ever found in western Europe.

Happisburgh, however, saved its greatest revelation until 2015. In the wake of another spring storm, a local photographer noticed slabs of newly exposed rock beneath the groynes of the beach that were pockmarked with what appeared to be human footprints. These were subsequently dated to around the same period as the flint tools and bones, more than 800,000 years ago.

The prints are believed to have belonged to a species known as *Homo antecessor*, or 'Pioneer Human', fossils of which had previously been found in Spain, but never this far north. Researchers identified the prints of five separate adults and children: a family group making their way in a southerly direction along the foreshore of the ancient river, which was back then fringed with forests of pine and birch.

In the era of Pioneer Human, Britain was a giant peninsula joined to mainland Europe by a tract of marsh and low ridges known as 'Doggerland'. Artefacts from this lost landscape have also been found on the beaches of Norfolk.

Eartham Pit Boxgrove, West Sussex

A disused gravel pit on the outskirts of Chichester does not, on the face of it, appear to be the kind of place you would expect to make discoveries capable of reshaping the way we view our distant past. But between the 1970s and 1990s, objects discovered at Eartham Pit, near the village of Boxgrove, did just that.

In a layer 20 metres (65 feet) below the surface of an old quarry, which around half a million years ago lay at the foot of a sheer chalk sea cliff, archaeologists discovered an extraordinary wealth of palaeolithic faunal remains. The bones of deer and wild horses, as well as long-extinct species of wolf, giant deer, bison, bear and rhino, were scattered across an area of land that had been buried under a layer of windblown sand soon after the remains had been deposited, around 480,000 years ago. This meant the items were preserved more or less exactly where they had been dropped – a great rarity.

Hundreds of stone tools were also found at Eartham Pit, among them exquisitely symmetrical hand axes of the 'Acheulian' type knapped from local flint. Analysis of scratches on the bones indicated the tools had been used to butcher the animals. The meat had then been removed to the edges of a nearby wood, on higher ground presumably less plagued by flies and the stench of rotting flesh, where it was consumed.

None of this, however, would have made national headlines had it not been for the discovery of two large fragments of a shin bone and a couple of teeth, which turned out to be from an early hominin known as *Homo heidelbergensis*. The tibia was from a left leg: its owner is estimated to have been 1.8 metres (6 feet) tall, weighed around 80 kilograms (176 pounds) and been very well built. Analysis of *H. heidelbergensis* skulls found in Germany and Greece suggest he would have had a large, jutting face, pronounced brows and a sloping forehead.

Physical anthropologists are still debating whether this species was an ancestor of modern humans, or a 'blind alley' in evolutionary terms. But the Boxgrove discovery remains significant for being the oldest hominin fossil ever found in Britain.

Quite how intelligent the *H. heidelbergensis* people at Eartham were is a matter of debate among palaeontologists. While some assert they scavenged their food, others claim the animals whose bones were discovered here were hunted. This is significant, because hunting requires a level of forward planning and social cooperation of which archaic humans would not theoretically have been capable due to the size of their brains.

Based on close analysis of the bones, however, the consensus today is that these people did indeed hunt, probably using wooden spears (examples of which have come to light in comparable sites on the Continent); and that to do so they must also have had some basic form of speech, because without the ability to communicate it would have been impossible to kill an animal as large as a rhino.

Perhaps the most convincing proof of all that this was more than a 'fifteen-minute' culture, living from moment to moment, are the beautifully balanced hand axes unearthed at Boxgrove. To make such items requires both dexterity and the ability to visualize something in advance. At one spot, more than four hundred axes were found, most of them apparently unused, suggesting they had been stockpiled. And if that is true, then these are people who were able to anticipate future needs – an important threshold in the cognitive development of humans.

Bifacial flint hand axe from Boxgrove.

Goat's Hole Cave Paviland, Gower Peninsula

In the autumn of 1822, reports reached the Talbot family of Penrice Castle on the Gower Peninsula, near Swansea, that an intriguing find had been made in a sea cave on their estate. A couple of local men had climbed at low tide into a cavity in the limestone cliffs near the hamlet of Paviland, where they found what appeared to be pieces of mammoth tusk.

Keen amateur antiquarians, the Talbots contacted the Reader in Geology at Oxford University, the Reverend William Buckland, who had made a name for himself writing about 'bone caves' and their significance. Buckland duly arrived in the Gower the following January and spent a week excavating the sediment lining the floor of the cave, where, among the bones of long-extinct animals, he made a discovery that would fascinate palaeontologists for generations: the partial skeleton of a human, stained by a vivid red ochre, which had been deposited with handfuls of periwinkle shells, ivory pins and a pierced tooth.

The 'trinkets' were interpreted as evidence the burial was that of a woman, most probably 'dating from the Roman period'. The red hue, asserted Buckland, indicated she was a 'prostitute or witch'.

In fact, tests carried out in 2009 showed that the so-called 'Red Lady of Paviland' was a young man who had died around 33,000 years ago, during a relatively warm interglacial spell in the Upper Palaeolithic. Back then, sea levels were 80 metres (262 feet) lower and the coast lay 100 kilometres (60 miles) further west. The pale blue-grey cliffs of the Gower rose from an undulating plain of tundra, buttressing the southern edge of a plateau roamed by woolly mammoths, rhinos, bison, giant deer, reindeer and horses. Competing with humans for this bounty were packs of hyenas, wolves and bears – species well adapted to the extreme cold that prevailed at these latitudes during those long interglacial winters.

Much speculation has surrounded the significance of this teardrop-shaped cave in the Gower, which is accessible for a few hours each day at low tide. While Neo-Pagans assert that it served as a shamanic or cult site and should be revered as such, archaeologists tend to interpret the presence of the bones as being the result of an unhappy accident: the young man probably died while hunting mammoths on the plains and was laid to rest here by his companions.

The bones of the 'Red Lady' are today preserved at the Oxford University Museum of Natural History.

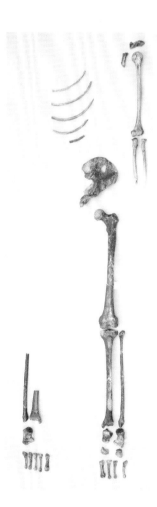

The red ochre staining the human remains found at Goat's Hole is believed to have been sprinkled on the body during the burial.

Creswell Crags Derbyshire

This little limestone gorge on the border of Nottinghamshire and Derbyshire is riddled with small caves whose floors have revealed traces of habitation dating back 40,000 years or more. Lured here by migrating reindeer and horses, its first occupants were Neanderthals, who left behind hand axes and simple tools (of the type classed by palaeontologists as 'Mousterian') made from flint, quartzite and claystone.

The most noteworthy finds, though, date from the warmer 'OIS 2 Interstadial' phase of the late Ice Age, which began 13,000 years ago and lasted for around a millennium, during which time average temperatures in Britain would have been slightly higher than they are today. *Homo sapiens* inhabiting Church Hole at Creswell adorned the walls of the cave with a dozen engravings of spirit or prey animals such as red deer, aurochs and bears. Only visible in certain light conditions, these had remained hidden in plain sight since the grottoes were first investigated in the late nineteenth century. Some had even been obscured by modern graffiti.

Of particular interest is a representation of a bison, discovered only in 2003. Bison were a species not present in Britain when the piece is believed to have been carved, suggesting the people who created it must have migrated from the Continent to what would then have been the southern limits of the great ice fields carpeting the north of Europe.

Several pieces of portable art dated to this period were also found at Creswell Crags, most famously the figure of a horse's head carved on to an equine rib bone.

Among the huge number of flint lithics discovered here were many originating from much further south in Britain. It seems the blades, which were usually trapezoidal in shape and are thought to have been attached to the ends of spears, had been knapped from larger cores discarded at their place of origin – presumably in order to reduce the weight the hunter-gatherers carried. Petroglyphic analysis has identified the Vale of Pewsey near Avebury in Wiltshire – around 320 kilometres (200 miles) away as the crow flies – as the source of much of the flint deposited in the caves of Creswell Crags.

The famous equine etching from Creswell, scratched on to a horse's rib.

Star Carr Vale of Pickering, North Yorkshire

The most important and intensively studied Mesolithic site in Europe, Star Carr, was discovered in 1948, when a farmer named John Moore spotted scatterings of what looked like flint blades in a drainage channel he was clearing on his land in the Vale of Pickering, North Yorkshire.

A series of trenches was cut, revealing other artefacts made of wood and antler. The acidity of the waterlogged peat at the site ensured that the items were exceptionally well preserved. Organic matter from the Mesolithic rarely survives, but over decades of archaeological digs at Star Carr a wealth of fascinating objects has come to light in a range of materials, offering vivid insights into the lives of the deer hunters who camped here around 9000 BC.

The definitive finds were twenty-one red deer skull caps, or 'frontlets', which had been adapted to be worn as headdresses. Leather straps would have tied them to the top of a person's head – whether as a hunting disguise or, more likely, for ritual purposes is unclear.

More certain, thanks to dendrochronological analysis of its timber, is that the site was used for around three centuries (between 8777 and 8460 BC) as a seasonal hunting camp in late spring and summer, coinciding with the migration through the area of red deer herds. People erected simple shelters and platforms – the oldest man-made structures ever discovered in Europe – on what was then the shore of an extensive reed swamp, spending months each year hunting deer, along with aurochs and pigs. Badgers, foxes, wolves and bears were also killed for their pelts.

These headdresses and elk antlers appear to have been deliberately placed in the shallows, perhaps as a propitiatory offering to the spirits of the animals hunted here. Star Carr is also the source of the oldest piece of art to have survived from the Mesolithic: a shale pendant elaborately engraved with a design similar to patterns found on objects from contemporary sites in modern-day Denmark, hinting at some connection between the two areas via Doggerland, which was not yet inundated at this time.

Objects from Star Carr are on display at York Museum but no trace of the site's archaeological importance survives above ground today. The birch and poplar trees that once fringed the lake have gone, and the water has been drained away.

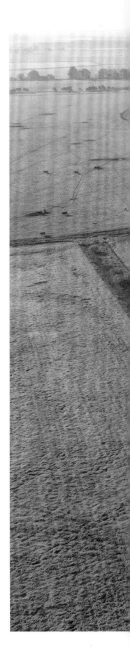

One of the famous antler headdresses discovered at Star Carr.

Cheddar Gorge Mendip Hills, Somerset

The Mendip Hills form an enormous limestone plateau between the River Avon and the Somerset Levels, with spurs and outcrops running west into the silty waters of the Severn Estuary. Today it is an upland of largely deserted, rain-soaked pasture, criss-crossed by drystone walls and old droveways that scythe over whaleback hilltops of bracken and bog overlooking lush green fields.

In the deep past, however, the Mendips presided over very different landscapes: expanses of glistening marshland dotted with islets, tropical swamps where hippos sloshed through the shallows, and icy tundra grazed by herds of woolly mammoths and rhinos. We know this thanks to the extraordinary vestiges of these distant epochs that have survived in caves honeycombing the limestone bedrock.

Fossilized in ancient sediment floors exposed by generations of local quarrymen and cavers, these include the bones of long-gone species of mammals laid down hundreds of thousands of years ago (such as lions, spotted hyenas and elephants), as well as tantalizing traces of early hominins. Bifacial flint tools, similar to those unearthed at Boxgrove and dated to 400,000–480,000 years ago, have turned up in caves at Banwell and Westbury-sub-Mendip.

The headline finds in the area, however, date to a more recent, warmer interlude at the end of the last Ice Age,
which began abruptly around 12,700 BC. Within an amazingly short time (perhaps as little as twenty years), *Homo sapiens* from what is now France appeared in the region, following the horse herds north and setting up camps in Cheddar Gorge.

Gough's Cave, on the east side of the defile, has yielded a particularly rich storehouse of artefacts from this period of the Upper Palaeolithic, including decorated tools made from red deer antler (believed to have been used for making rope and string), elaborately engraved rib bones and pebbles, and the earliest traces ever found in Britain of domesticated dogs.

The well-preserved skeletal remains of two adult humans and two children were also uncovered here. Microscopic analysis of cut and scrape marks on the bones has revealed the corpses were expertly skinned and butchered shortly after death. Eyes, tongues and brains were removed, and some of the larger bones cracked open to expose the marrow.

Some have interpreted this as evidence of cannibalism, for which parallels exist in modern times among groups in the Highlands of New Guinea. Others have pointed out no hard proof actually exists for the consumption of human flesh at Gough's Cave, and that the excarnation and bone breaking could just as plausibly have been a ritualized way of disposing of, and venerating, the remains of loved ones.

Aveline's Hole Mendip Hills, Somerset

Human settlement around the Mendip plateau of Somerset ceased with the return of cold conditions at the tail end of the Ice Age, roughly 11,000 years ago. When this freeze ended, Mesolithic hunter-gatherers reoccupied the region, pursuing wild horses, red deer and aurochs.

In addition to a massive quantity of flint flakes, blades and arrowheads scattered at temporary camp sites across the uplands, a unique hoard of human remains from this period has been discovered at Aveline's Hole, a cave in Burrington Combe, on the north side of the Mendip Hills. Unlike at Gough's Cave (see previous spread), the cavern does not appear to have been inhabited. Instead, it was used as a kind of tomb, where bodies were ceremoniously laid to rest, some covered in tufa stones found at local springs, others adorned with perforated horses' teeth, fragments of ammonite fossils and red ochre. One had a piece of a child's skull placed on her shoulder; a stalagmite had formed on another. Engravings have also been identified on the walls of the cave, which is nowadays locked to protect its prehistoric rock art.

In total, more than fifty different individuals are represented in what is often described as 'Britain's oldest cemetery'. While much of the skeletal material was sadly lost when the museum in Bristol where it was displayed was destroyed in a bombing raid in 1940, enough survived to be able to carry out modern radiocarbon dating tests and DNA analysis.

The results were significant. Firstly, they confirmed a very early date of 8500–8300 BC for the Mesolithic bones, placing them as exact contemporaries of 'Cheddar Man' – Britain's oldest complete skeleton – found in Gough's Cave. DNA extracted from his remains has shown that the first Mesolithic inhabitants of the Mendips were dark skinned, had green, blue or hazel eyes and brown, curly hair, and were lactose intolerant. DNA tests on the Aveline's Hole material have also revealed that this influx formed part of a wider population movement originating in southeast Europe and the Near East, starting around 12,700 years ago and which reached the periphery of northwest Europe in the ninth and tenth millennia BC.

Most surprising of all was the discovery among the bones of two fragments of skulls dated to 3800–3700 BC – the Early Neolithic period. This was nearly five thousand years after the Mesolithic bodies were placed in the cave, corresponding to the period when the first herder-farmers were settling in the region. Genomic tests on the Neolithic cranial pieces pointed to very different origins for these people: in Iberia and southern France, associating them with a wave of migration originating in the Mediterranean rather than the Danube and Pontic-Caspian steppe.

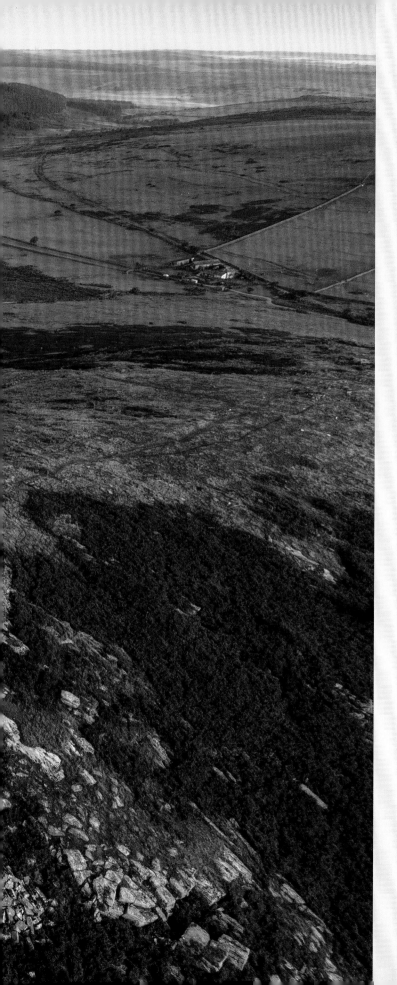

Neolithic Britain

Prehistory is replete with forgotten pioneers, whose exploits are remembered only by inference. And so it is with the dawn of the Neolithic era in Britain, a period when a relatively small number of individuals imported new knowledge and tools from mainland Europe that both transformed the landscape of Britain and brought to a close a way of life that had held sway since the end of the last Ice Age.

This quiet revolution began sometime towards the end of the fifth millennium BC. No one can say for certain when or where, but at some point a group of Neolithic mariners on a beach in what is now northern France climbed aboard a boat (probably made of hide and tar, or possibly wood) and paddled it towards the white cliffs on the horizon.

By this time, Britain had been an island for more than two thousand years. Its indigenous Mesolithic population had led a largely nomadic existence little altered since the retreat of the glaciers. The possibility that it was they who first crossed the Channel in canoes cannot be ruled out. But given the absence from the archaeological record of any Mesolithic craft capable of navigating the open seas, let alone transporting livestock, we must assume the direction of travel was south to north, in substantial crafts of a kind depicted in rock art at Neolithic sites in southern Brittany (which by this time we know maintained trade connections across Biscay and beyond).

First Landfall

The pioneers would have taken with them supplies of dried, salted and smoked meat (probably a mixture of pork, mutton and beef) sliced with finely knapped flint blades, along with supplies of emmer wheat and barley carried in woven baskets or terracotta pots. For hunting, they used long bows made from yew and hazel wood that unleashed arrows tipped with leaf-shaped shards of flint. They may also have taken axes of beautifully shaped and polished stone – highly valued objects made from rock quarried in auspicious places and passed down through generations, which may have been believed to hold magical powers.

Thus equipped, our Neolithic pioneers would have probed the British coastline in search of suitable places to camp and hunt, returning on subsequent expeditions with breeding animals and urns of seed grain with which to establish settlements. Judging by the very early

Stowe's Pound, Bodmin Moor, Cornwall

radiocarbon dates yielded by Coldrum Long Barrow in Kent (3960–3880 BC), the lower Thames region appears to have been their first landfall.

Precisely what motivated them to brave one of the world's most treacherous seaways (and potentially the wrath of the people whose territory they colonized) one can only guess. Perhaps competition for grazing land caused by population increase or climate change, or the approval of a culture that rewarded exploration?

The Early Neolithic (4000–3500 BC): Axes, Herds and Urns

Considerable debate has raged among archaeologists over how exactly the ensuing process of 'Neolithization' occurred in Britain. One side propounds a theory of 'diffusion': that the new package of technologies and knowledge was introduced by small numbers of migrants, then selectively adopted and shared across the rest of the island by its indigenous inhabitants. The other school of thought attributes the spread to successive waves of migration involving larger numbers of emigrants, principally from the Paris Basin and the Morbihan region of southern Brittany. Proponents of the latter cite as proof the similarities between Early Neolithic monuments (and the artefacts found in them) dotted along the Atlantic coast of Europe, from Galicia to Ireland and the Orkneys.

Improvements in dating techniques have tended to favour the mass migration theory, but the process is likely to have been a complex mixture of the two, varying from region to region through time. What we can say with a high degree of probability – by comparing finds and radiocarbon dates from disparate sites across northern France and Britain – is that four distinct waves of settlement occurred in the first two centuries of the fourth millennium BC, beginning in southeast England around the Thames Estuary, followed by movements from Normandy to the Solent, and from Brittany to Cornwall, Wales, and coastal Scotland and Ireland.

Once established, this new culture worked its way inland via the river systems. Britain in the Early Neolithic was carpeted by old-growth, deciduous forest, travel through which would have been more difficult than navigating the rivers in shallow-draft boats, which is why the Thames, the Wiltshire Avon and the Stour, in particular, appear to have been major conduits for initial exploration and settlement.

Analysis of pollen and snail shells in soil samples taken from the earliest Neolithic sites indicate that some forest clearance took place around this time, probably to open up land for grazing and herding, and for planting cereal crops. Once the soil had been exhausted, new ground would have been cleared, leaving the old patches to regenerate.

Tombs and Sacred Circles

Special clearings were also created on hilltops as venues for communal gatherings. Edged by segmented circles of ditches and banks, sometimes adorned with wooden posts, these so-called 'causewayed enclosures' are known to have hosted funerary rites, in which bodies were sometimes defleshed and left in the open to be cleansed by the elements. Objects such as antlers, fragments of animal bone, knapped flint and pottery were also deposited in pits and ditches as offerings. Some enclosures may also have hosted blood sacrifices and

The Giant's Grave, Gower Peninsula

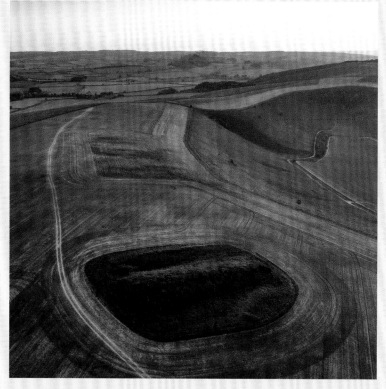
Long Barrow, Cold Kitchen Hill, Wiltshire

gift exchange ceremonies, when kinship ties would be reaffirmed and, perhaps, marriages brokered or conducted, accompanied by feasting and beer drinking.

The other class of monuments associated with the Early Neolithic era are 'long barrows'. Erected mostly on hill crests and near rivers, these communal tombs comprised chambers of wood or stone enclosed inside earth (or turf) mounds. Though the nature of the beliefs underpinning them remains obscure, it is likely they were the focus of ancestor veneration. Ancestors may have been regarded as supernatural beings capable of protecting the living from evil (or causing evil if not properly respected), and ensuring the health of livestock and success of harvests.

Precisely how long after the early waves of Neolithic migration from the Continent such monuments were constructed continues to be a subject of debate, but it is possible the individuals whose remains they held were from the generation of pioneer settlers and their close

descendants. In this way, these 'houses of the dead' symbolized the durability of ancestral lineages, reinforcing a claim to land that had been hard won through tree felling and possibly even conflict with its previous occupants.

The Middle Neolithic (3500–3000 BC): 'Boom and Bust'

By 3400 BC community tombs had started to decline in favour of individual burials, initially in large, long mounds but later in smaller, oval or round ones, as well as pits and ditches in older enclosure monuments. Inhumation also became less common through the second half of the fourth millennium BC, replaced by cremation burial.

A question that has long exercised archaeologists specializing in the Neolithic is the extent to which the disappearance of chambered tombs may have reflected changing social patterns during this era. Environmental evidence suggests that cereal cultivation diminished rapidly through the thirty-fourth and thirty-third centuries BC. Forest clearings regenerated and settlements began to appear in areas of poorer soil, showing that pastoralism was now more important than it had been previously. Could it be that the old kinship ties connecting families to their ancestral land through patterns of patrilineal inheritance and endogamy (marrying within the clan) had weakened as extended families became more dispersed?

Climate change has been advanced as a possible explanation for this 'boom-and-bust' episode in the Neolithic. Weather conditions are known to have deteriorated in the thirty-fourth century BC, with cooler winters, wetter summers and an increase in Atlantic storms coinciding with what astrophysicists refer to as a 'grand solar minimum' – a protracted phase of reduced solar activity that impacted the earth's climate.

Alternatively, the demographic decline in and dispersal of Britain's early farming populations may have been due to ecological overreach. Yields from newly opened land will have fallen away sharply after a decade or two in many areas.

Along with the demise of chambered tombs and causewayed enclosures in Britain came the rise of a new kind of ceremonial monument called the 'cursus'. Much larger in scale, these long circuits of parallel ditches with enclosed, squared-off ends ranged in extent from a few hundred metres to ten kilometres. The precise nature of the beliefs and rituals associated with them are not well understood, but most were carefully aligned with the sunrise or sunset of the winter or summer solstice, as well as with pre-existing ancestral long barrows.

The Greater Cursus, Wiltshire

was later established; see p. 50) around which twenty 'mini henges' were excavated in the Middle Neolithic period.

Henges grew larger and more complex over time, with higher banks, deeper ditches and bigger circumferences. It seems that, in tandem with the demise of cereal crops and the development of a more nomadic-pastoralist way of life, there arose the need to congregate in large numbers at auspicious times of the year. Henges became the venues for these mass gatherings of dispersed communities, where rites associated with death and the solar cycle were performed. Camp grounds to accommodate the influx sprang up where feasts and perhaps livestock markets were held, establishing a juxtaposition of 'domains of the dead' and 'domains of the living'.

The most striking example is Stonehenge, where an earth circle 110 metres (360 feet) wide was dug around 3000 BC on open ground to the south of the Greater Cursus. Within this have been found an array of pits, known as the Aubrey Holes after the archaeologist who first excavated them, which may (or may not) have been sockets for bluestones (spotted dolerite) brought from the Preseli Hills of West Wales. More certain is that the earthwork served as a major cremation ground – where bodies were ritually burned and the ashes buried – both in the Aubrey Holes and surrounding ditch.

Around five centuries later these bluestones were moved and a circle of colossal trilithons added; while in nearby Durrington Walls, a few miles northeast, a second, even larger earthwork with giant banks was carved above the River Avon, enfolding the largest settlement in Neolithic Britain, close to the spot on the river where people who had travelled to Salisbury Plain by boat would have alighted. The huge quantity of animal bone (mostly from pigs) discovered here, alongside substantial timber circles, suggest that rituals and feasting took place on a grand scale as part of winter solstice ceremonies focused on nearby Stonehenge.

Enormous rocks were quarried and transported, sometimes over long distances, and installed in circular enclosures or henges. Like the castles and cathedrals of medieval Europe, they would have been expressions of the power and identity of their creators, as well as giant astronomical instruments tracking the movement of the sun and moon.

These monumental sites have also been interpreted as reflecting the emergence of a more hierarchical society, ruled by clans or hereditary chiefs. The building of henges and stone circles required a coordinated effort by many people. Whoever or whichever group

The Late Neolithic (3000–2400 BC): Monumental Landscapes

The later phase of the Neolithic period in Britain saw the emergence of extensive ceremonial landscapes. Earth circles with large standing stones started being built on a scale not seen since the megalithic creations of southern Brittany centuries earlier. Archaeologists are divided over whether the practice originated in West Wales, the Orkneys or Wessex, but it was embraced by communities across Britain, notably at Avebury in Wiltshire, Thornborough in Yorkshire, the Lake District and the Scottish Highlands and Islands.

The precursor for stone circles was the 'henge' – a circular enclosure comprising outer banks and inner ditches – which frequently appears alongside or near cursi. A prime example of this is the Greater Cursus on Salisbury Plain (one of two in the area where Stonehenge

Silbury Hill, Wiltshire

initiated the construction of sites such as Stonehenge and Brodgar was clearly capable of co-opting a sizeable workforce. Surplus food would have had to have been stockpiled, indicative of a society that had moved well beyond a mere subsistence economy, and which had the time and resources to devote to large-scale building projects.

That this population maintained far-reaching travel networks with a wider world we know from the way the cultural phenomenon of stone circle-building spread as far north as the Orkney Islands. In turn, the distinct forms of Orcadian domestic architecture influenced the style of dwellings built at places like Durrington Walls on Salisbury Plain. The classic Late Neolithic 'Grooved Ware' pottery also originated in the Orkneys centuries before it was widely adopted in Wessex, suggesting sustained interaction between disparate regions of Britain.

By now established for over a thousand years, trade networks in the Neolithic were the conduit for commodities as well as ideas: amber from the Baltic and rare kinds of stone, such as jet, shale, callaïs and jadeite, used to make jewellery and polished stone axes. Exotic substances and intoxicants too were traded and used in rituals.

It was by means of these long-distance trade routes that new ideas and technology imported to northwest Europe in the early second millennium BC by settlers with Eurasian steppe ancestry first began to enter Britain. Their arrival – dubbed 'the Beaker Revolution' – would herald a dramatic turnover in population and the gradual emergence of a way of life based on land enclosure and the family home rather than monument building – a transformation vividly revealed through aerial photography.

The Sweet Track Shapwick Heath, Somerset

In 1970, while digging at the Eclipse Peat Works on Shapwick Marshes in the Somerset Levels, a peat man named Ray Sweet unearthed with his mechanical digger a tangle of blackened planks and posts. Correctly deducing from their depth that these must have been of great antiquity, he dispatched samples to a team of archaeologists from Cambridge. Further investigation revealed that the timbers formed part of a walkway 4 kilometres (2½ miles) long connecting what would, six thousand years ago, have been two islands surrounded by a watery swamp. Dendrochronological analysis showed they came from trees felled between 3807 and the winter of 3806 BC, making them among the earliest Neolithic artefacts discovered in Britain.

The wood, mainly oak and lime, came from the (then) islands of Westhay and Shapwick Burtle. Flint mined in distant Sussex, 225 kilometres (140 miles) to the east, was used to make the axes and wedges deployed to split and prepare the timber, which had been secured in place using thousands of pegs and rails.

Fifteen years of archaeological work in the peat beds subsequently revealed an extensive network of other plank-and-wattle walkways, uncovering the existence of a unique way of life in the Levels that endured well into the Iron Age. Stone axes and arrowheads, fragments of finely made pottery, yew and hazel bows – and possibly even a child's toy axe – were found preserved in the acidic peat.

The greatest treasure of the 'Sweet Track', though, is undoubtedly a polished stone axe head found carefully inserted beside one of its planks, perhaps as an offering. The object was made of polished green jadeite, quarried near the summit of Monte Viso in the Italian Alps. Although no one can be sure of the beliefs framing this votive act, the symbolism of the phallic stone embedded in the fecund marsh is obvious.

The axe head and other finds from the area are displayed in the Museum of Somerset in Taunton. To preserve them, the timbers were left where they were found, buried deep in the old peat workings. You can see what the original would have looked like by visiting a reconstruction near the Avalon Marshes Centre.

Nowadays on display at the Museum of Somerset in Taunton, the Sweet Track Axe was deliberately pushed into the bed of the marshland, probably as an offering.

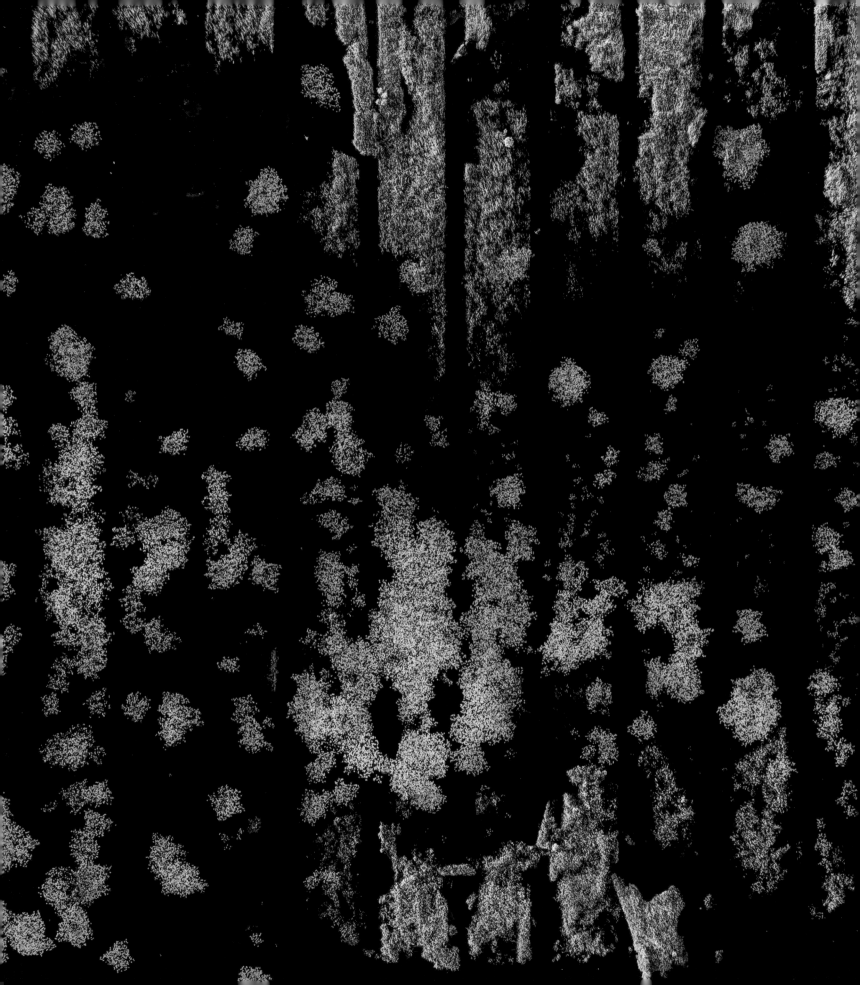

Windmill Hill Avebury, Wiltshire

Windmill Hill, half an hour's hike across the fields north of Avebury, is both the largest and most comprehensively studied causewayed enclosure in Britain.

For many years after it was first excavated by Alexander Keiller in the 1920s, the site came to define the material culture and ritual activity of the Early Neolithic period in Britain. Keiller identified three concentric circles on the hilltop, ranging from 90 to 360 metres (295 to 1,180 feet) in diameter. Radiocarbon dating indicates these were dug over a span of roughly two generations, beginning in 3685–3635 BC, and remained in use for 180–200 years.

The nature of the ceremonies performed on the hill is suggested by a wealth of pottery finds and bones (both human and animal) deposited in the segmented, roughly circular ditches. The artefacts (many of which have been successfully radiocarbon dated) included cattle, sheep and goat remains, the skeleton of a baby, the skull of a three- to four-year-old child, the hind legs of a toad, a dog's jaw and numerous pieces of red deer antler, presumed to have been used as digging tools.

Feasting may well have taken place here intermittently, at a time when the great chambered tomb at nearby West Kennet was in use. It is safe to assume that the people whose bones were placed in that tomb belonged to individuals who would have gathered here for annual festivals, perhaps with families from other settlements to meet, trade gifts, trade livestock, broker marriages and resolve conflicts. The setting certainly lends itself to marking rites of passage. Although diminutive by the standards of British uplands, the hill boasts a sweeping 360-degree view over the Kennet Valley's hinterland of shadowy chalk ridges and its numerous long barrows.

It takes just over half an hour to walk from Windmill Hill to the Great Henge at Avebury (see p. 106) – a trek along an ancient trackway best undertaken before dawn, when the downs to the south and east are invariably wreathed in mist.

West Kennet Long Barrow Avebury, Wiltshire

Marooned amid the furrows like beached whales, thirty
Neolithic long barrows are to be found in the vicinity of
Avebury. Around half of them were lined with stone, where
remains of the dead were enclosed in chambers accessed
via central passages. Occurring from Spain to Sweden,
these 'chambered tombs' are a defining feature of the Early
Neolithic landscape in western Europe. The best known
nestles on a hillside south of Avebury. Measuring 100 metres
(328 feet) from head to tail, West Kennet Long Barrow was
constructed using a mix of local sarsen (a kind of diamond-
hard sandstone that occurs naturally as half-buried boulders
in the chalklands of southern England) and softer, honey-
coloured oolithic limestone, which must have been quarried in
the Bath–Frome area and carried here up the Vale of Pewsey.

Skilled masonry was required to build the walls and
ceiling of the central passage measuring 12 metres (39 feet)
in length, with chambers opening off it, in which bones
from an estimated thirty-six men, women and children
were interred, the majority between 3670 and 3635 BC.

Bodies were probably placed inside fully articulated and
left to decompose, whereupon the bones would have been
removed and rearranged according to age and gender, with
adult males in the westernmost corner and young people
in the southeast transept. Others were placed here 'clean'
from the start, having been defleshed and purified nearby.

The communal effort required to build such a structure
must have been considerable, underlining the reverence
with which people in the Early Neolithic held their
ancestors. The anthropomorphic nature of these ancient
tombs is also striking. The deceased were, in effect,
returned to a womb in the sky that served as a portal to the
underworld where the spirits, gods or ancestors could be
contacted and appeased. Seen from below, they may have
provided quiet reassurance to people as they went about
their lives, reaffirming the legitimacy of their ownership
of the land. From above, the resemblance of long barrows
to the polished stone axes beloved of Britain's first farmers
is also revealed.

All Cannings Down Alton Barnes, Wiltshire

Ceremonial monuments from the Neolithic period often maintained lines of sight with others, creating webs of inter-visibility that endure to this day. A prime example are the prehistoric vestiges dotted along on the southern edge of All Cannings Down, a breezy chalk upland to the south of Avebury, whose hill crest affords sweeping panoramas over Pewsey Vale to Salisbury Plain.

The focal points here are a pair of causewayed enclosures, dramatically sited on projecting spurs. To the east, Knap Hill rings a prominent hilltop, while 3 kilometres (1.8 miles) west, Rybury Camp occupies an even more pivotal location, which was fortified during the Iron Age. Both have been reliably dated to the early thirty-sixth century BC, a hundred years or so after the first phase of West Kennet.

Between the two sits a massive chambered long barrow known as 'Adam's Grave'. Just over 70 metres (230 feet) in length, the trapezoidal tomb is less intact nowadays than some of its more famous cousins around Avebury, but offers a striking spectacle nonetheless, its edges flanked by deep ditches from which the soil used to build it was extracted. The track threading between these three sites must have been in constant use since the Neolithic, and may have provided a kind of ceremonial pathway looping from Avebury over the chalk downs and back to the Kennet River, via a string of other tombs and mortuary enclosures. Many archaeologists specializing in the period believe this was the route along which the great sarsen stones used in the construction of Stonehenge were pulled across All Cannings Down.

The Vale below also holds some significant ancient remains, including the 'mega henge' at Marden, and no less than eight extraordinary middens dating from the Late Bronze Age/Early Iron Age. The enormous piles of cattle, goat, sheep and pig bones dotted across the valley floor bear witness to what must have been ceremonial feasts involving hundreds of people. Herders from upcountry might have converged in the Vale to sell livestock at annual fairs. Human bones interred among them suggest the middens were not merely rubbish heaps but also of some ritual significance. Their scale is astonishing: one below Rybury held bones from around five thousand separate animals.

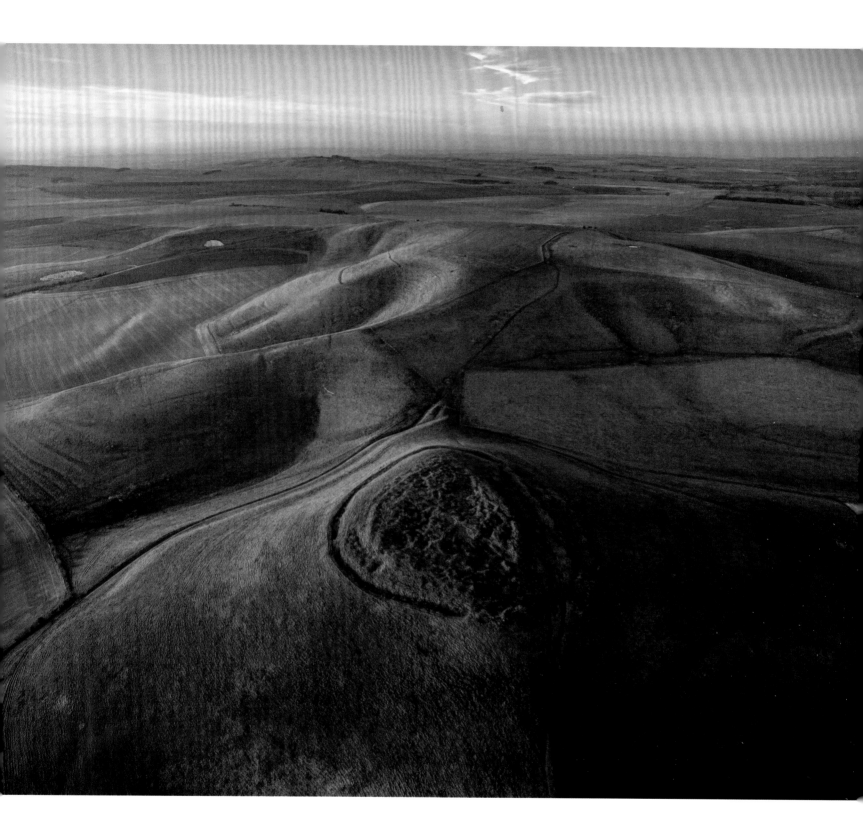

The Trundle Goodwood, West Sussex

The coastal plain around Chichester in West Sussex is believed to have been among the first areas colonized by Neolithic herders from the Continent. More easily accessible from the tip of the Normandy peninsula than points further west, its shoreline of estuaries, meandering rivers, creeks and marshes, backed by a line of what would then have been densely forested hills, would doubtless have appealed to prospective settlers from across the Channel.

That they were here at the end of the fifth millennium BC we know from pollen and mollusc analysis, which shows that limited, short-lived forest clearance occurred around this time. More tangible evidence of Neolithic settlement litters the crest of the South Downs in the form of flint mines, long (and oval) burial barrows and a sequence of at least eight causewayed enclosures. Of these, the Trundle, on St Roche's Hill, overlooking Goodwood Racecourse, has yielded some of the earliest dates and most interesting finds.

It is not hard to imagine why our Neolithic ancestors might have selected the hilltop as a sacred site. Rowing across the Channel, or paddling around the backwaters of what is now Chichester Harbour, the hill would have appeared as the most distinctive landform for miles. From its brow, dramatic views extend across the coastal lowlands to Portsmouth, the Isle of Wight and out to sea, as well as northwards over the misty valleys of the Weald.

The Trundle (from the Old English *tryndle* meaning 'circle') has received considerable attention from archaeologists since 1925, when its outlines were first spotted in aerial photographs. E. C. Curwen identified two circuits and a segmented spiral ditch within the more

prominent Iron Age fortifications. Subsequent excavations revealed a mass of struck flint, animal bone, some unusual carved chalk blocks, a bone phallus and sherds of pottery. Carbonized residue on one of the latter was dated to 4040–3770 BC, placing the site at the very start of the Neolithic period in Britain.

Finds from the Trundle are displayed at the Barbican Museum in Lewes.

White Sheet Hill Kilmington, Wiltshire

Offering the only practicable routes through the primeval forest covering most of Britain at the start of the fourth millennium BC, rivers were far more central to life in the Early Neolithic period in Britain than they are today. So it is unsurprising that the headwaters of rivers leading from the heart of the chalk uplands to the sea were the object of great reverence in prehistory.

A perfect example is White Sheet Hill, near the Stourhead Estate in Wiltshire, where a pair of causewayed enclosures overlooks the headwaters of the Rivers Wylye and Stour. Surrounded on three sides by steep escarpments, the site feels like a pivotal point in the local landscape, with wide-ranging views that would have formed an inspirational backdrop for feasting and ceremonies.

Analysis of snail shells in the soil show that the circles originally formed clearings that overlooked the treetops to a forested vale below. Archaeological work conducted ahead of a pipe-laying project in 1989–1990 revealed a mass of animal bone, pottery and charred hazelnuts in the ditches of the segmented southern enclosure, which was originally 4 metres (13 feet) deep. Radiocarbon dates point to 3595–3540 BC for the creation of the ditch, placing it

as a contemporary of the more famous enclosures on Hambledon Hill, a day's walk to the south.

Hambledon was by far the most extensive and richest Early Neolithic complex in the Wessex chalklands. Excavated by Roger Mercer and his team between 1974 and 1982, the hill revealed an unparalleled wealth of detail about how causewayed enclosures were used and what their broader significance might have been.

Compacted chalk provided the surface of Hambledon's main enclosure, where bodies were dismembered and defleshed using flint scrapers before being left to the elements and local scavengers. Once cleansed, the bones were removed and interred in nearby burial pits or chambered tombs.

Could the twin enclosures on White Sheet have been used for similar rites? Given the similarity of the landforms, it would not be inconceivable, though since the northern circle has never been investigated, hard evidence is lacking. It is possible that the dead from here were conveyed to Hambledon, reinforcing the hierarchical status of regional enclosures that some archaeologists have suggested may have been in play at the time.

Pimperne Long Barrow Cranborne Chase, Dorset

Little evidence of settlement from the Early Neolithic period has come to light on Cranborne Chase, the large chalk plateau to the east of Hambledon Hill. But the upland was clearly important when it came to honouring the dead. The area retains a particularly rich crop of funerary monuments, the most impressive of them a giant long barrow in the fields outside Pimperne, on the western flank of the Chase.

This behemoth among chambered tombs, thought to be the largest of its kind in England at over 112 metres (367 feet) in length, would originally have occupied a woodland clearing. It has never been excavated, but doubtless encases the remains of a cross section of the local community. The barrow would in its day have been capped with a layer of gleaming white chalk, surrounded by large, segmented ditches (long since filled), and perhaps a wood-fenced area where the bodies would have been defleshed and laid out prior to interment in the tomb.

Over the succeeding centuries, Neolithic barrows on Cranborne Chase grew more modest in scale and tended to hold fewer individuals, the overwhelming majority of them men. Often interpreted as a shift towards a less egalitarian, more male-dominated society, this trend is exemplified by the famous Wor Barrow, 19 kilometres (12 miles) northwest of Pimperne on Handley Down. The burial mound, which dates from the Middle Neolithic, was first excavated by Augustus Pitt Rivers in the nineteenth century, who discovered inside it three complete male skeletons and the disarticulated remains of three others (also men). Nearby, a pair of much smaller, Late Neolithic round barrows held separate, articulated, male skeletons buried with grave goods (in one case a beautiful shale belt), prefiguring a trend that saw its fullest expression in the Early Bronze Age barrow cemeteries of Wessex, a fine example of which lies a couple of fields away from the Wor Barrow on Oakley Down (see p. 135).

The Greater Cursus Wiltshire

The only cursus still clearly visible at ground level in Britain scythes across open pasture to the north of Stonehenge, on high ground connecting the River Avon and its tributary, the Till. Sometime halfway through the fourth millennium BC, Neolithic people cut parallel trenches over this chalkland, running 2.8 kilometres (1¾ miles) between two large, conspicuous long barrows. Roughly midway along it, the so-called 'Greater Cursus' dips where it is bisected by a shallow, dry combe that would once have held a seasonal stream, or 'winterbourne'.

Fragments of antler picks found at the bottom of the ditches dug to create both the Greater Cursus and the long barrow at its western terminal were radiocarbon dated to 3770–3660 BC, as was material excavated from the 'Lesser Cursus', a smaller circuit of 400 metres (1,312 feet) located nearby. We can't be sure which came first, but the ensemble was clearly some kind of processional complex associated with the dead, which people walked as a form of ritual.

Work on this scale, involving hundreds of people and a high degree of social organization, had never been undertaken before in these islands, which begs the question of what prompted our ancestors to invest so much labour?

The Greater Cursus may conceivably have followed a route sacred to the Mesolithic people who erected large timber posts on this plateau centuries before (close to the site of the stone circle). Some have also posited a link to the environmental changes taking place at the time these monuments were dug: soil and mollusc analysis has shown that woodland clearance in the region stopped midway through the fourth millennium BC, when communities seemingly deserted their traditional territory and gave up cereal cultivation in favour of nomadic pastoralism. Population also appears to have dropped.

One explanation for this 'Neolithic Collapse' is that a marked decrease in solar activity around this time led to a fall in average temperatures. Another posits a connection with the demise of the Neolithic Yamnaya 'mega settlements' of eastern Europe in this period, which many researchers now believe may have been the result of the world's first pandemic. Traces of the bacteria *Yersinia pestis*, an ancestor of the microbes responsible for bubonic plague, have been found in numerous Neolithic graves. Could it be that this same pathogen was having an impact on the inhabitants of Salisbury Plain, and that the Greater Cursus was an attempt to halt the spread of disease by placating or appeasing the gods?

Knowlton Circles Cranborne Chase, Dorset

By 3300 BC causewayed enclosures had been largely abandoned and circular burial enclosures had taken their place as the principal ceremonial centres. Comprising an inner ditch and outer bank, these 'henges', as we now know them, were often sited close to rivers or in natural amphitheatres. Entry tended to be via one or more causeways, often (but not always) aligned with seasonal movements of the sun.

One of the best-preserved examples in the country sits at the southern edge of Cranborne Chase, on a low hilltop edged by red earth banks. Overlooking these, our Neolithic ancestors created an oval, wood-fenced mortuary enclosure that was later upgraded to a henge – the first of four constructed on the site.

In the backyard of a farm on the nearby main road are fragments of the largest of them: a 'mega henge' measuring 250 metres (820 feet) at its widest point. The real show stealer at Knowlton today, however, is 'Church Henge', a fully intact, 100-metre (328-foot) ditch-and-bank earthwork named after the twelfth-century chapel the Normans later erected in the middle of it – a remarkable cultural assemblage spanning more than four thousand years of religious building.

Knowlton sits at a geological fault line where the chalk of the Chase gives way to the Tertiary gravel and greensands of the coast – of which Neolithic famers would have been well aware. Access to the sacred site would have been most easily gained by boat via the River Stour and River Allen. The latter flows to within a few hundred metres of Knowlton. Pilgrims would have alighted at the foot of the red Pleistocene cliffs (eroded traces of which survive) and proceeded uphill along a trackway whose route is now followed by a country lane.

Knowlton was also a major burial site in the Early Bronze Age: a huge collection of barrows litters the surrounding fields. Most are only visible as crop marks today, but one particularly large specimen, the 'Great Barrow', still stands just to the west of Church Henge, at the centre of a large ditch-and-bank circle that may originally have been a fifth henge monument.

Crickley Hill Birdlip, Gloucestershire

If you were a Neolithic pioneer scouting for a camp ground overlooking the Severn Vale, Crickley Hill, on the outskirts of what is now Gloucester, would have been your landform of choice. A prominent spur of crumbling oolithic limestone, it is flanked on two sides by deep, forested valleys and has what must rank among the most exotic views in Britain.

That Mesolithic hunter-gatherers congregated on the triangular hilltop we know from the discovery of bone fragments radiocarbon dated to between 4375 and 4230 BC. Several centuries later, sometime in the first few decades of the thirty-seventh century, a pair of concentric causewayed ditches was dug around the hillcrest, enclosing a central cobbled-stone platform where rituals involving fire and depositions of bone, pottery, flint and antler appear to have taken place.

Subsequently overlaid by a succession of cairns and stone circles, this 'shrine' was approached via a 100-metre (328-foot) walkway, lined by limestone slabs and timber palisades. Such a sophisticated assemblage clearly attracted unwanted attention midway through the fourth millennium BC, when one of the gateways into the enclosure was seemingly attacked and torched. Hundreds of typically Neolithic 'leaf' arrowheads were discovered among the charred remains, which some archaeologists have claimed as evidence of Britain's first battle. Evidence of a similar attack at a site in Dorset around the same time suggests that the thirty-fifth century BC may have been a period of conflict.

Today, Crickley is maintained as a country park, easily accessible by car and popular among Gloucester residents as an escape from the city. Dominating the right side of the photograph opposite, its Iron Age ramparts are more conspicuous than its Neolithic vestiges these days, but come at dusk, when the sun is sinking behind the shadowy profile of the distant Malvern Hills, and the place feels every inch a site of great antiquity.

Belas Knap Long Barrow Winchcombe, Gloucestershire

Nestled on the crest of Cleeve Hill above the village of
Winchcombe in the Cotswolds, Belas Knap – from the
Old English for 'beautiful' (*belas*) and 'view' (*cnaepp*) – is a
textbook chambered tomb of the 'Cotswold-Severn' type.
At 50 metres (164 feet) in length, it is on the large side for
the region, but exhibits the classic trapezoidal shape and
deep forecourt flanked by rounded 'horns', where funerary
rites are believed to have been conducted.

Inside, four separate stone-lined chambers held bones
of more than forty men, women and children, most of them
radiocarbon dated to the Early Neolithic, between 3700 and
3600 BC, placing them in the same period as the earliest
enclosures on Crickley Hill (see previous spread).

Aside from its enigmatic walled-off entrance
(interpreted by some as a 'portal for the spirits'), the long
barrow is known for having yielded examples of distinctive
elongated (dolichocephalic) skulls. The Victorian craniologist
John Thurnam was the first to draw a correlation between
these and the Neolithic period, noting that specimens from
chambered tombs tended to be of a different shape to those
found in later Beaker burials (whence his oft-quoted adage
'long barrows, long skulls; round barrows, round skulls').

The observation has been borne out by more recent
cranial studies, although whether the older, elongated skull
type was a genetic trait (as Thurnam asserted) or the result
of head binding in infancy remains a matter of debate.
DNA research has, if anything, swayed the argument in
Thurnam's favour by suggesting that the arrival in Britain
of Beaker culture around 2450 BC precipitated a dramatic
turnover in the gene pool: within three centuries, indigenous
Neolithic ancestry appears to have been largely replaced by
genomes derived from continental Europe and the
Eurasian steppe.

Uley Long Barrow Uley, Gloucestershire

Among the more substantial Early Neolithic long barrows nestled on the rim of the Cotswold scarp is this chambered tomb above the village of Uley. Its nickname – 'Hetty Pegler's Tump' – derives from that of the wife of the man who owned the field in the seventeenth century, when, as now, the tomb huddled in the lee of mature woodland, screened from the westerlies that regularly blow up the Severn Vale.

In its heyday, the barrow would probably have enjoyed a fabulous uninterrupted view – one that will have been maintained by tree clearance in the Early Neolithic, and which can only be approximated with aerial photos such as the one opposite, shot looking southwest over Cam Long Down and Dursley towards the Welsh coast.

When it was first excavated in the nineteenth century, the mound was shown to hold a transepted gallery with four chambers, from which a total of twenty-three mostly articulated skeletons were removed, along with sherds of Early Neolithic pottery and numerous animal teeth.

Several similar tombs of the Cotswold-Severn type rest on nearby hillcrests (including one at nearby Nympsfield, and another on the brow of Selsley Common) but this is the best preserved. Roofed and walled with the original megaliths, the interior can still be accessed on hands and knees.

Also worth a visit in this area is Uley Bury, a large Iron Age hillfort a mile or so to the south. Its huge ramparts, dating from the third or second century BC when this was the domain of the Dobunni tribe, offer a fine walk with sweeping vistas.

Stoney Littleton Long Barrow Wellow, Somerset

Stoney Littleton, near the village of Wellow in northeast Somerset, may not be the largest of the surviving long barrows in this region, but it is one whose location, overlooking a serene valley on the southern fringes of the Cotswolds, often inspires return visits. The surrounding landscape would have been more densely forested when it was built in the Early Neolithic period, and the open ground would not have been enclosed by hedgerows as today's fields are. But the contours of the valley can have changed very little over the intervening fifty-six or fifty-seven centuries. Sitting atop the earth mound on a summer's evening, with grasshoppers and butterflies flitting through the long, bleached grass that grows on the tomb, it is easy to forget the city of Bath lies just over the hill.

The classic trapezoidal shape is still very much in evidence, along with the horned courtyard typical of the Cotswold-Severn-style tomb. Thanks to renovation work carried out in 1999, you can now crawl along the central gallery, flanked by three pairs of alcoves, to the end chamber, which is illuminated by the rising sun on the morning of winter solstice.

Adorning the left door jamb is a splendid Jurassic ammonite, doubtless discovered in the fossil-rich fields hereabouts when the tomb builders were scouting for slabs of Blue Lias and Forest Marble to use as building material. Its placement is one of those little touches that beautifully bridges the eras, reminding us that pretty views and natural curiosities appealed to our distant ancestors every bit as much as they do to us.

Chûn Quoit St Just, Cornwall

Some of the strongest evidence that settlers from southern Brittany travelled by sea to the western fringes of Britain early in the fourth millennium BC are the many and striking similarities between monuments of the Morbihan region with those in the far west of Cornwall and Wales.

'Portal dolmens' are a prime example. Known in Wales as 'cromlechs' and in Cornwall as 'quoits', these quirky structures are essentially chambered tombs centred on a stone box or 'cist' made of worked slabs. The difference between them and more common tomb types from the Early Neolithic is that their centrepiece was a giant capstone, set on three or four uprights. Boulders with huge, bulbous tops were selected and their undersides 'pecked' flat using round rocks as hammers. The megaliths, which weighed upwards of 70 tonnes, would then be manoeuvred into position –

probably by as many people as could be gathered together from the local community. The result seemingly defies the laws of physics.

Occupying a tract of open moorland that falls away to a patchwork of ancient Celtic fields, Chûn Quoit is a particularly beautiful specimen. Its location was clearly chosen for its far-reaching views, which today encompass a landscape that has changed very little since the Bronze Age.

Writing in the nineteenth century, local antiquarians describe the dishevelled remnants around its base of what may have been a giant cairn. These stones now form an uneven pavement poking through the turf, but it is unlikely they were part of the original construction, unlike the weathered cup marks chiselled across the top of the capstone, which can be seen from above.

Pentre Ifan Nevern, Pembrokeshire

The most iconic of the many portal dolmens in the far west of Wales is this elegantly constructed cromlech at the foot of the Preseli Hills in north Pembrokeshire. Unlike Chûn Quoit in Cornwall (see previous spread), whose interior face was chiselled flat, the level underside of Pentre Ifan's 5-metre (16-foot) capstone seems to have been formed by splitting the boulder. It was probably too large to drag, leading archaeologists to speculate that the megalith may originally have been a glacial erratic, dumped on this sea-facing hillside by melting ice at the end of the Pleistocene. A pit in the earth nearby of a similar size lends credence to this theory.

As for the original appearance of the tomb, a study has suggested that rather than forming the core of a huge, 30-metre (98-foot) drystone cairn, as was traditionally thought, the assemblage we see today remains largely as it was intended to look, with the capstone seemingly afloat on three tapering uprights. The sight of the huge boulder delicately balanced in such a way certainly casts a spell, especially when viewed silhouetted against the morning sun with the crags and bracken of Carn Igli illuminated to the west.

The Welsh Stonehenge?
Directly above Pentre Ifan is a moorland pass known as 'Tafarn y Bwlch' where numerous large standing stones, overlooking the sources of the area's two main rivers, flag what would have been an important route across the Preselis in ancient times. From the peat bogs on its northern side rise the remnants of a large stone circle dating from the Late Neolithic (roughly 3000 BC) which some archaeologists believe may have been the original home of the Stonehenge bluestones.

Only four monoliths remain in situ from a once large complex estimated to have been 110 metres (360 feet) wide – the same size as the original earthwork at Stonehenge and

the only other one in the country with this diameter. Five empty sockets have been discovered where large stones once stood. Known as 'Waun Mawn', the site is now believed to have formed the hub of one of the most important religious centres in Neolithic Britain, encompassing two causewayed enclosures and at least seven long barrows.

Showery Tor Bodmin Moor, Cornwall

A sombre feel hangs over the heart of Bodmin Moor, a 260-square-kilometre (100-square-mile) tract of desolate moorland in central Cornwall. Few of the millions who pour across it en route to the white-sand beaches further west spare a second glance through their car windows at its undulating expanse. But the moor holds one of the richest storehouses of prehistoric remains in Europe, including many from the Early and Middle Neolithic periods, when herding communities occupied these now deserted uplands.

Stone rows, propped boulders, orthostats (standing stones) and circles are widely distributed across Bodmin's peat bog and bracken. Research carried out over the past few decades suggests that far from being randomly placed, most were carefully aligned with prominent 'tors' – the outcrops of weathered granite that crown most moorland hills hereabouts.

Rough Tor (pronounced 'row', as in 'dispute'), in the far north of Bodmin near Camelford, appears to have been of particular significance. Sometime in the Early Neolithic, its summit rocks were encircled by a low drystone wall, interpreted as an enclosure demarcating a sacred space. That the rocks dotted along the ridge above were revered in the distant past can also be inferred from the huge ring cairn at the base of Showery Tor, ten minutes' walk along the hillcrest to the north. Here, a blue-grey granite outcrop weathered into an extraordinary shape was honoured with thousands of stones, carried to the hilltop more than 5,500 years ago and placed as votive offerings.

It is easy to imagine that people believed the tors to be the work of ancestral spirits or mythic beings, whose exploits may have been described in stories handed down through generations. Or perhaps our Neolithic forebears propitiated the spirits present in the hills as atonement for the clearing of trees and scrub from lower elevations – for the 'gift' of land?

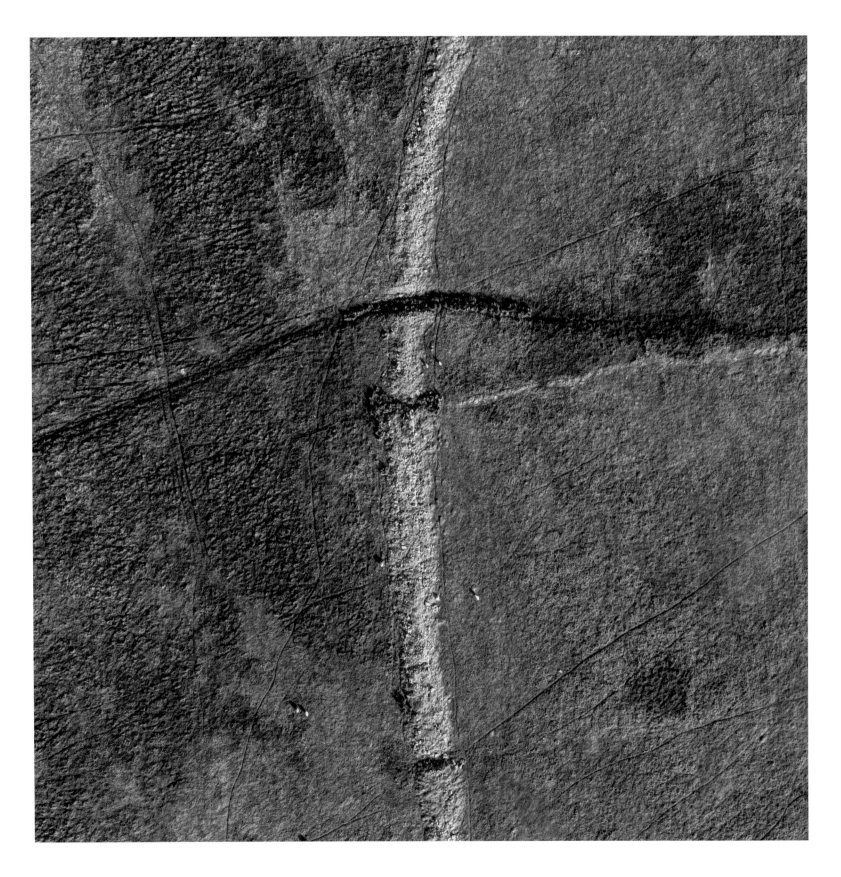

The Long Cairn Rough Tor, Bodmin Moor, Cornwall

Rough Tor's pivotal role in the ritual landscape of Neolithic Bodmin becomes more apparent if you explore the moors on foot. A standing stone on an ancient trackway, for example, may flag the spot where the tor first comes into view on a ridge line. Propped stones and stone rows frequently point to it, and two prominent stone circles sit at its base. Conversely, monuments are noticeably thinner on the ground in areas where views of the sacred peak are obscured – so-called 'sight shadows'.

The most remarkable of all these alignments is a long drystone cairn scything across the western flank of Rough Tor itself. Easily mistaken for an ancient field boundary, the structure stretches for over half a kilometre (a third of a mile) across grass and bracken, bending at two points to line up with the most prominent rock outcrops indenting the skyline above. Close examination of breaches in it made during army manoeuvres in World War II have revealed that the cairn was carefully constructed, with a layer of turf sandwiched between courses of stone.

It is likely the platform may have served to guide people to the summit of Rough Tor, heightening the drama of the approach. In Tibet, 'mani walls', made of pebbles inscribed with sacred Buddhist mantras, serve a similar function at the entrances to villages and monasteries. Pilgrims walk around them in a clockwise direction, adding their own carved prayers to the wall for good luck as they pass. Whether or not something similar happened here in the Neolithic it is impossible to say for sure, but this is definitely one ceremonial site where the reverence our distant ancestors felt for the natural landscape and spirits residing in it becomes palpable.

Bryn Celli Ddu Llanddaniel, Anglesey

Separated from the Wessex chalklands by hundreds of miles of mountains and rivers, the Neolithic people of northwest Wales appear to have maintained closer contact with communities in Ireland than with the inhabitants of southern England. Evidence for this is the emergence of a distinctive style of passage tomb on the island of Anglesey, of which the finest and most intriguing is Bryn Celli Ddu, near the Menai Strait.

The site started life around 4000 BC when Mesolithic hunter-gatherers erected five timber posts in what would then have been a woodland clearing. A thousand years later, Neolithic herder-farmers excavated a henge monument on the same spot, with an outer ditch and inner bank enclosing a circle of seventeen standing stones. In its centre, a pit was dug in which a human ear bone was deposited along with a richly carved slab of limestone covered in swirling, serpent-like shapes reminiscent of rock art at Newgrange in Ireland (a copy remains in situ, the original having been taken to the National Museum of Wales in Cardiff).

Sometime in the Bronze Age, around 2000 BC, the standing stones were smashed or pushed over and a passage grave built inside the henge, which was then heaped with earth. A ring of kerbstones shows the extent of the original mound, which was considerably larger.

Reconstructed in 1929, the stone-lined passage tomb can be entered to reach a central chamber, where a pillar of blue schist – possibly a fossilized tree trunk – is the focal point. This inner space is illuminated by the sunrise of the summer solstice – another feature connecting it with Ireland, where such alignments were common.

More recent archaeological research has also identified more than a dozen cup-mark Neolithic carvings on rocks around Bryn Celli Ddu, which is believed to have formed part of a wider ritual landscape incorporating two other passage graves in the area.

Barclodiad y Gawres Rhosneigr, Anglesey

A prominent headland fringed by cliffs and transparent, turquoise water would seem an obvious place to site a tomb. In fact, Neolithic burials in Wales rarely occur so close to the seashore as this (reconstructed) chambered tomb midway between Rhosneigr and Aberffraw, on Anglesey's southwest coast.

Barclodiad y Gawres (Welsh for 'Full Apron of the Giantess') is unusual in another respect: when excavated in the 1950s, the cruciform cavern at its heart was found to contain several large orthostats inscribed with horizontal bands, spirals, lozenges and chevrons, connecting it stylistically both with nearby Bryn Celli Ddu (see previous spread) and the art adorning the great tomb of Newgrange in the Boyne Valley, Ireland.

This link with the Irish Neolithic should come as no surprise. To have got here from Brittany in the early fourth millennium BC, pioneering herder-farmers must have been skilled mariners. The Irish coast lies just over 100 kilometres (66 miles) west as the crow flies – only 16 kilometres (ten miles) more than the shortest crossing (between Strumble Head in Pembrokeshire and Rosslare) – which would have made southeast Ireland far more easily accessible by boat from this stretch of coast than, say, the chalklands of southern England.

The decorated slabs, with their intriguing geometric designs, nowadays reside in a domed concrete bunker covered in turf, built to replace the original tomb, which was dismantled in the 1950s during archaeological work. In the middle of the central chamber, excavators also unearthed residue from some kind of burned offering comprising wrasse, eel, grass snake, hare, mouse, shrew and various amphibians – a stew subsequently buried under a pile of carefully placed limpet shells and pebbles.

On a raised knoll overlooking a pair of pretty white-sand coves, the site is easily reachable via the coast path and boasts expansive views over the Menai Strait to the hills of the Llŷn Peninsula.

Langdale Axe Factory Cumbria

Trade or gift exchange was conducted over surprisingly long distances in the Neolithic period. Firm evidence for this is the distribution across Britain of polished stone axes originating in quarries located a long way from where they were discovered. Modern petroglyphic analysis has enabled archaeologists to identify the precise locations of several of these and, intriguingly, nearly all of them were high, prominent mountain peaks.

The source of around one third of all the polished axes discovered in Neolithic contexts across Britain was a phalanx of rock towers, or 'pikes', towering over Great Langdale in the Lake District. These dramatic landforms must have held special significance for our distant ancestors, because they went to extraordinary lengths to cut from them a rare kind of silica-rich, volcanic tuff.

Reaching veins of this stone would have been a perilous undertaking – no more so than in the case of one shallow cave on Pike o'Stickle (the summit on the left of the massif featured opposite), where it is still possible to view the holes and chipping marks left by prehistoric stonecutters. 'Roughouts' of crudely shaped rock have been found here – rejects discarded during the initial shaping, which was carried out in situ before the best pieces were removed for polishing at lower, safer altitudes. Aside from making the stone more beautiful to hold and look at, polishing improves the strength of the axe (sharp corners and other defects increase stress concentrations, making breakages more likely).

Once finished, Langdale axes found their way to all four corners of the British Isles, though it seems they were particularly prized in Lincolnshire and East Yorkshire, where a large number have come to light.

A semi-worked 'roughout' of a stone axe, discovered amid the scree in a gulley below Pike o'Stickle, where it was quarried around 5,000 years ago.

Grime's Graves Thetford Forest, Norfolk

It is hard to overstate the importance that flint must have had for people in the Neolithic age. Made of microscopic quartz crystals formed when pockets of silica, derived from decomposed sponges and other marine life, were compacted inside seabed sediment, the rock can be splintered to form razor-sharp cutting blades, which were used for a variety of purposes: from making weapons, slicing meat and scraping hides to fashioning toolkits of knives, awls and wood axes. Flint occurs naturally as nodules on the surface across the chalklands of southern England, but the best stuff – a black, treacly, glass-like form that was more durable – is found mostly below ground.

Of the nine Neolithic mines so far discovered, eight lie on the chalk downs of Sussex, Hampshire and Wiltshire. The most highly prized flint, however, came from a site further northeast – in Norfolk. Set in a clearing of lumpy heathland surrounded today by the pines of Thetford Forest, Grime's Graves holds the remnants of 433 shafts, dug 14 metres (46 feet) vertically down through the chalk to the valuable 'floorstone' flint below. Archaeologists have estimated that each 12-metre (39-foot) wide shaft would have taken teams of twenty men around five months to excavate. The spoil they removed was dumped inside older, redundant openings. Low-roofed galleries supported by wooden pillars fanned out from the base of the pits, following the flint seams sideways.

Enough rock was removed from Grime's Graves in the Chalcolithic period – between 2600 and 2300 BC, when the site was at its most productive – to create hundreds of thousands of axes. Examples have been discovered as far away as Cornwall and the Lake District. Today, the site is managed by English Heritage, whose excellent guided tours include access to two of the shafts.

Cairn Holy Creetown, Dumfries and Galloway

'Chambered cairns' are a type of funerary monument found along the length of Europe's Atlantic coast, from Iberia to Shetland. Archaeologists tend to focus on the stylistic differences between them, but the similarities are arguably more significant, not least for the implication that regions widely separated by expanses of ocean were interconnected five to six thousand years ago, and that there must, by inference, have been maritime routes and a seafaring culture by means of which people were routinely able to navigate the Bay of Biscay, English Channel and Irish Sea.

A prime example of the 'Clyde' or 'Clyde-Carlingford' style of chambered cairn, prevalent in the southwest of Scotland, rests on a balcony of high ground overlooking Wigtown Bay in Dumfries and Galloway, near Cairn Holy Farm. Sometime in the early fourth millennium BC, a community of herder-farmers found this area of level ground, probably by following Kirkbridge Burn inland from Dirk Hatteraick's Cave on the coast. Surrounded on three sides by moorland ridges and open to the sea on the fourth, the site enjoys fine views that on clear days take in the Isle of Man and the distant Cumbrian Fells.

The spot was chosen as the site of two impressive stone-lined tombs. The larger of the pair, known as Cairn Holy I, was fronted by a facade composed of eight tall, slender monoliths, arranged in a shallow semicircle. Flanking the main entrance like a group of sombre mourners, these stones still retain great presence, especially on bright, moonlit nights.

Flakes of jadeite from the Italian Alps and silky black pitchstone from the Isle of Arran were unearthed beneath what archaeologists have identified as hearths in the 'forecourt' next to the megaliths, where ceremonies are believed to have been conducted. By the time Stuart Piggott and Terence Powell dug here in 1949, however, the substantial capstones and heaps of rock that would originally have enclosed the structure had long been pillaged by local farmers for use as building material.

Some compelling theories into the possible connections between the monument with its wider setting have been posited by local resident Joseph Proskauer, an American tourist who fell in love with the site after visiting it in the 1990s and settled here. Joe has since spent more than three decades studying the movement of shadows across the stones and alignments with points on the horizon where the sun, moon and constellations rise and set at significant moments in the calendar, concluding that the monument was a work of genius by a Neolithic Galileo.

The fact that many of these phenomena would have been visible only from the interior chambers, where bones of the Neolithic dead were interred, suggests the whole installation may have been a kind of complex gift for the ancestors, rather like the practice of leaving grave goods.

Rubha an Dùnain Isle of Skye

One of the singular pleasures of discovering prehistoric sites in Britain is the chance to experience the often strikingly beautiful landscapes in which they reside. Our distant ancestors clearly had an eye for places blessed with fine outlooks and distinctive atmospheres, and this is particularly true of a remote, rock-studded peninsula on the southwest fringe of Skye, where in the Neolithic era people erected a pair of stone-covered chambered cairns beside a small lochan.

Encompassing the Isle of Rùm on one side and the chocolate-covered gabbro pinnacles and razorback ridges of the Cuillin Hills on the other, the views from Rubha an Dùnain are mesmerizing. When cloud shadows pass across the ocean, Soay Sound turns from lapis blue to an inky-purple colour, while at dusk the mountains inland momentarily glow molten red.

The tip of the promontory is only accessible on foot, via a 13-kilometre (8-mile) out-and-back walk from the campsite at the foot of Glen Brittle. Skirting a beach of black volcanic sand and a string of pebbly coves, the path climbs steadily on to the headland before winding down via the ruins of an old farmstead to the peaty waters of Loch na h-Airde, on the north shores of which nestle the pair of cairns.

Pottery fragments unearthed in the forecourt of one during a dig in the 1930s suggests Neolithic origins, although Beaker sherds from the Early Bronze Age appear to have been inserted at a later date into the polygonal chamber inside. The undisturbed portions of the tomb-cairn still have their covering of turf and heather, while the short passageway retains its original drystone walls.

Remnants of Mesolithic occupation have been found in a nearby rock shelter, but it is for the vestiges of an eleventh-century Viking harbour that Rubha an Dùnain is nowadays most renowned. A canal was cut from the lochan to the sea to ensure water levels remained high enough for birlinn-style boats to access a stone-lined quay, overlooked by one of the best preserved Iron Age sea forts in Scotland. The footprints of numerous Viking farm cottages also survive around the lake – an area that remained inhabited by members of the MacAskill clan until the 1860s, when the land was cleared.

The Camster Cairns Caithness

With its open expanses of blanket bog, dark conifer forests and myriad peaty lochans and pools, the Flow Country, on the opposite side of the Pentland Firth from Orkney, could be a stretch of Siberian tundra. In the first half of the fourth millennium BC, however, this corner of windswept northern Caithness enjoyed a warmer, drier climate. Populations of Early Neolithic herder-farmers grazed their livestock in the uplands, leaving in their wake a scattering of impressive stone monuments. Among the most striking is a pair of chambered cairns, reached today via a ribbon of potholed tarmac.

Measuring more than 70 metres (230 feet) in length, the larger of the two basks on the high ground like a recumbent reptile: slender and trapezoidal in shape, with low, horned facades at either end enfolding what were probably ceremonial forecourts.

Two narrow passageways pierce the structure. You can crawl through them to enter the chambers inside, surmounted by corbelled roofs (nowadays fitted with fibreglass domes to allow the light in). It is thought this long cairn may originally have been two separate round ones that were merged at some point in the distant past.

A second, smaller cairn to the southwest also holds an inner chamber which you can squeeze into on your hands and knees. Both monuments have been renovated and fitted with iron grilles to keep the local sheep at bay. Boardwalks provide easy access across the surrounding bog from the roadside.

The significance of this site is thought to have been its proximity to the source of one of the Flow Country's major streams, Camster Burn, which meets the sea at Wick harbour.

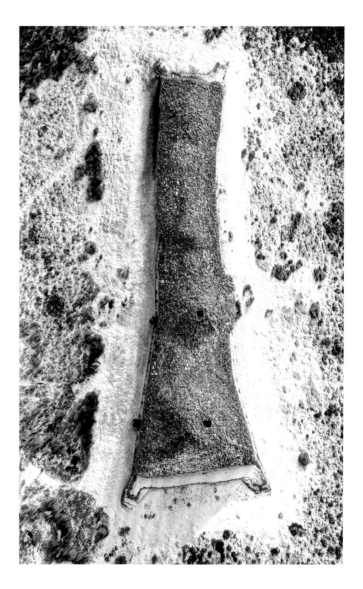

Maeshowe Orkney

Towards the end of the fourth millennium BC, a few centuries before the first circle of bluestones was erected at Stonehenge, the Orkney archipelago off the northeast coast of Scotland witnessed a remarkable flowering of Neolithic culture. On a par with the great megalithic sites of Avebury and Stonehenge, the islands' ancient architecture is unique in its style, variety and scale.

Wood was as scarce back then as it remains on the islands today, so the ancient Orcadians made good use of stone for construction, elevating its use to a high art form. Ranging from grey-tan and reddy-pink sandstones to speckled basalt and camptonite, the island's rocks offered a broad palette of different colours and properties, which the prehistoric builders exploited to great effect.

The chambered tomb of Maeshowe, near the southeast shores of Loch Harray, has long been regarded as the high-water mark of Neolithic monument building in Orkney. Similar in outline to its larger cousin at Newgrange in Ireland, the structure was erected around 2800 BC, perhaps on top of a pre-existing stone circle. Large, weathered megaliths that may previously have served as menhirs (standing stones) were incorporated into the central chamber, which is roughly square (or, rather, cruciform) in shape, and spanned by a vaulted, beehive roof resting on large corner buttresses.

When first opened by (a rather heavy-handed) amateur archaeologist, James Farrer, in 1861, the cavity was found to contain no human remains. Indeed, it may never have served as a tomb at all, but rather as a sophisticated light chamber used for ritual purposes. At sunset on the winter solstice, the last rays of daylight shine down the long, low-roofed entrance passage, momentarily illuminating the west wall of the inner sanctum – a spectacle these days relayed around the world via live webcam.

From the air, the earth platform on which Maeshowe stands, encircled by a ditch and low wall, creates an anchor point for the wider landscape. As with many Neolithic ceremonial sites, the hills encircling it form a natural amphitheatre around the flat, grassy plain, with its patchwork of fields and drystone walls, while to the west the stone circles of Stenness and Brodgar (see overleaf) rise sentinel-like from either side of the isthmus of land known as 'the Ness'.

Brodgar Orkney

One of Britain's greatest stone circles, the Ring of Brodgar sits at the heart of Orkney, surrounded by low hills. To the south a patchwork of tiny crofts, green pasture and glinting sea loch are bounded by summits of Hoy, snow-capped for much of the winter. On either side shimmer the glassy expanses of Lochs Harray and Stenness, their surfaces reflecting the luminous, ever-changing Orcadian sky.

Standing in this wondrous spot feels like being in a kind of sanctuary. It was surely the feeling of being in a hidden world, screened from the mainland by the hills yet open to the heavens and ocean, that appealed to the Neolithic people who settled here 5,500 or more years ago, and who would later construct the most remarkable ceremonial complex of its era in this northern archipelago.

Just twenty-seven of the sixty megaliths that originally formed the Ring survive, set in a circle 103 metres (340 feet) in diameter. They originated in at least seven different quarries from around the islands, perhaps representing the different communities who would have gathered at the site.

Excavations carried out in 2008 revealed the fact that the stones were placed in relatively shallow sockets. It seems size mattered more than durability to the ancient Orcadians, suggesting the clans who transported the megaliths from their home territories may have been in competition with each other. Alternatively, the fact that the holes had to be carved from solid bedrock rather than earth may account for their lack of depth.

Surrounding the circle is an impressive ditch, cut with red deer antler picks to a depth of over 4 metres (13 feet).

Building the henge involved the removal of around 11,000 tonnes of rock – a massive undertaking believed to have been carried out in stages over several decades, sometime around 3000 BC.

The Ness

A few hundred metres southwest of the Ring, the Ness of Brodgar was the site of the most sensational archaeological discovery in Britain for a generation. In 2002, a large complex of Neolithic religious and domestic structures, edged by a colossal wall, was uncovered on the narrowest stretch of the isthmus.

In scale, appearance and sophistication, the compound, which archaeologists are still unearthing from beneath the mantle of Orkney machair, has no known equivalent in northwest Europe. It appears to have evolved over a period of six centuries, from roughly 3300 BC, during which time new buildings were erected over the ruins over older ones and their associated middens.

In addition to numerous structures, a wealth of artefacts has come to light, ranging from polished axes and beautiful mace heads made from Lewisian gneiss and speckled granite, to skilfully carved stone balls, items of jewelry, polished flint tools, geometric inscriptions and a mountain of animal bone – much of it originating in what appears to have been an Early Bronze Age feast when a herd of cattle was culled as part of a some kind of decommissioning event, following which the Ness fell into disuse.

The King's Men Stone Circle Rollright, Oxfordshire

'Stumps and lumps of leprous limestone' was how the eighteenth-century antiquarian William Stukeley described the megaliths of the King's Men circle – a characterization that still resonates today. Standing shoulder to shoulder behind a screen of wispy larch trees, the seventy-two stones have been weathered by millennia of wind and rain into gnarled, contorted shapes, whose bulges and cavities are embellished with patches of ancient lichen (one of which is at least eight centuries old).

The monument dates from the end of the Neolithic period, around 2400 BC, and lies adjacent to the prehistoric trackway connecting east and west England. Strong stylistic similarities between the circle and those of distant Cumbria – notably Castlerigg (see p. 92) and Swinside (see p. 97) – suggest a connection with the north, perhaps reflecting the importance to the people who lived here of the exchange or trade in polished stone axes from Langdale, examples of which have been discovered across the region.

The local oolithic limestone would have been too brittle to use for felling trees, and axes of stronger stone must have been highly prized, both as utilitarian and cult objects. This spot on a high Jurassic ridge in the heart of the country may well have been an important centre for long-distance trade. Ceremonies attracting participants from across Britain may have taken place here at auspicious times of year, such as the winter and summer solstices; feasting, initiations and marriages may also have occurred alongside the rituals, as they are believed to have done at Stonehenge and Avebury in the same period.

Close to the King's Men circle, the remnants of an Early Neolithic portal dolmen attest to the importance of the site perhaps as early as the thirty-eighth century BC. Lithic scatters unearthed in the area show it was also used long before that as a seasonal camp site by Mesolithic hunter-gatherers.

Arbor Low White Peak District, Derbyshire

High on Middleton Moor in the White Peak District of Derbyshire, Arbor Low is the best preserved and most impressive henge monument in the Pennines. It rises from the crest of a plateau of rolling limestone uplands whose wide-ranging views and loess soils would have appealed greatly to herders and farmers in the Neolithic period, when the first monuments were created here. A sprawling patchwork of drystone walls and green pasture, the area is still dominated by sheep farming and remains a rich storehouse of prehistoric sites.

Measuring 79 metres (259 feet) at its widest point, the bank-and-ditch henge is roughly oval in shape with causewayed entrances to the northwest and southeast. Inside it sprawl more than fifty limestone slabs, added several centuries after the henge was dug, their tops facing outward as if blown over by capricious giant. Opinion is divided over whether these megaliths originally stood upright or were intended to be recumbent. Either way, they make a unique and powerful spectacle when viewed from above, their pale-grey faces forming a striking star shape against the close-cropped turf.

A short walk across the fields to the southwest, an Early Bronze Age barrow rises from the remains of a much older oval tomb dating from the Early Neolithic period, in which pottery and human remains were discovered in the nineteenth century. The assemblage, known as the 'Gib Hill Double Barrow', was probably the first monument on this site, although field walking has yielded a mass of flint arrowheads discarded by hunter-gatherers during the Mesolithic.

Material recovered from Arbor Low and environs is divided mostly between the British Museum and Weston Park Museum in Sheffield. The latter holds the area's outstanding find: a wonderfully intricate necklace made from over four hundred pieces of polished Whitby jet and decorated bone found in the Bronze Age grave mound of a woman a short way northwest of the henge. She had been buried in a crouched position with a four-year-old child placed behind her shoulders. Radiocarbon dates indicate the necklace was two or three centuries older than the woman – perhaps a treasured heirloom?

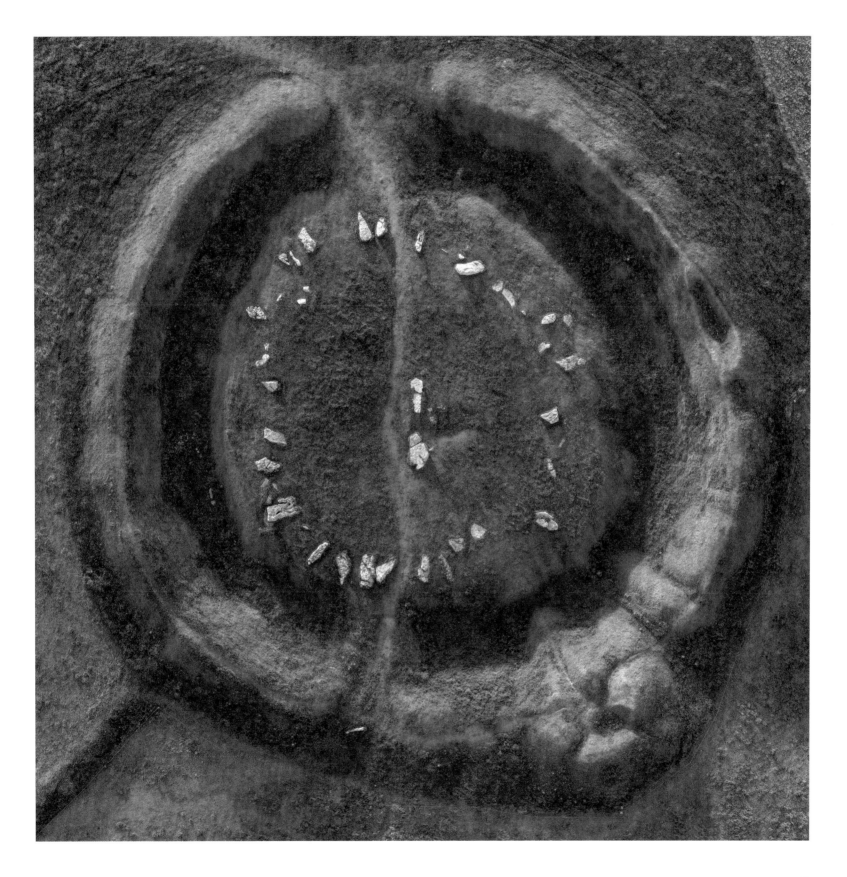

Castlerigg Cumbria

This much-visited stone circle owes its popularity to its dramatic setting, amid a natural amphitheatre of mountains at the heart of the Lake District. Whether streaked with snow or wreathed in early summer mist, Skiddaw, Blencathra, High Seat and Helvellyn form an epic backdrop to what is thought to be among the oldest megalithic circles in Britain, dating from around 3200 BC, when the region was exporting large numbers of polished axes made from stone quarried in Langdale (see p. 74).

A total of forty-two megaliths once stood on the site, of which thirty-eight remain in situ – four of them part of a 'cove' in the centre. Two of the largest guard a prominent entranceway on the north side of the enclosure, which was laid out in the form of a flattened circle, roughly 30 metres (97 feet) in diameter.

Castlerigg attracts a constant flow of admirers, so to make the most of its vivid atmosphere, aim to arrive in the early morning, when the grassy platform on which it stands is bathed in low sunlight and long, evocative shadows stretch towards the surrounding fells.

Swinside Cumbria

Tucked away in a remote valley on the southwest side of the Lake District, Swinside (aka 'Sunkenkirk') receives considerably less attention than Castlerigg (see p. 92), though it is comparable in terms of both design and atmosphere. The circle retains most of its fifty-five original standing stones, which form an oval 27 metres (93 feet) wide, entered via a well-defined opening flanked by prominent guardian stones on its southeast side.

No archaeological work has been carried out here since 1902, when little of note was discovered beyond the fact that the Late Neolithic makers of the circle levelled the grassy platform to create a kind of ceremonial plinth.

The Henges of Eamont Bridge Cumbria

If any monuments in Britain could be said to epitomize the disregard with which the creations of our pre-Roman ancestors have been treated by subsequent generations, it is this trio of henges on the south side of Penrith in the Eden Valley, Cumbria. One has been robbed of its megaliths; another is hemmed in by houses and motorways; while a third has been ploughed into oblivion.

Despite, or perhaps because of, such travesties, the site is well worth a detour. It may nowadays be difficult to discern amid the roar of traffic and creeping conurbation, but the significance of the location derives from its proximity to a narrow point in the Eamont River, which for many thousands of years served as a crossing point for travellers heading through the Eden Valley, which divides the uplands of Cumbria from those of Westmorland.

It was here, near the confluence of the Eamont and the Lowther at Mayburgh, that the region's Neolithic inhabitants created a huge henge made from river stones. An estimated 20,000 tonnes of different-colour pebbles were removed from the nearby beds and piled up to make a bank 3 metres (10 feet) in height, encircling an area 117 metres (383 feet) in diameter. Blue-black, white and red were the colours favoured, which must have made for a striking spectacle.

Mayburgh Henge has long since lost all but one of the large monoliths believed to have stood in its centre, but remains in a far better state of preservation than the nearby

King Arthur's Round Table, 400 metres (a quarter of a mile) east across the fields, which is sliced on two sides by roads.

A third henge, called the 'Little Round Table', lies 200 metres (just over 650 feet) further south. Partly buried under tarmac and cement, or ploughed out, its once massive banks and ditches are now difficult to discern, but 4,500 or more years ago would have formed a prominent part of a remarkable ceremonial landscape.

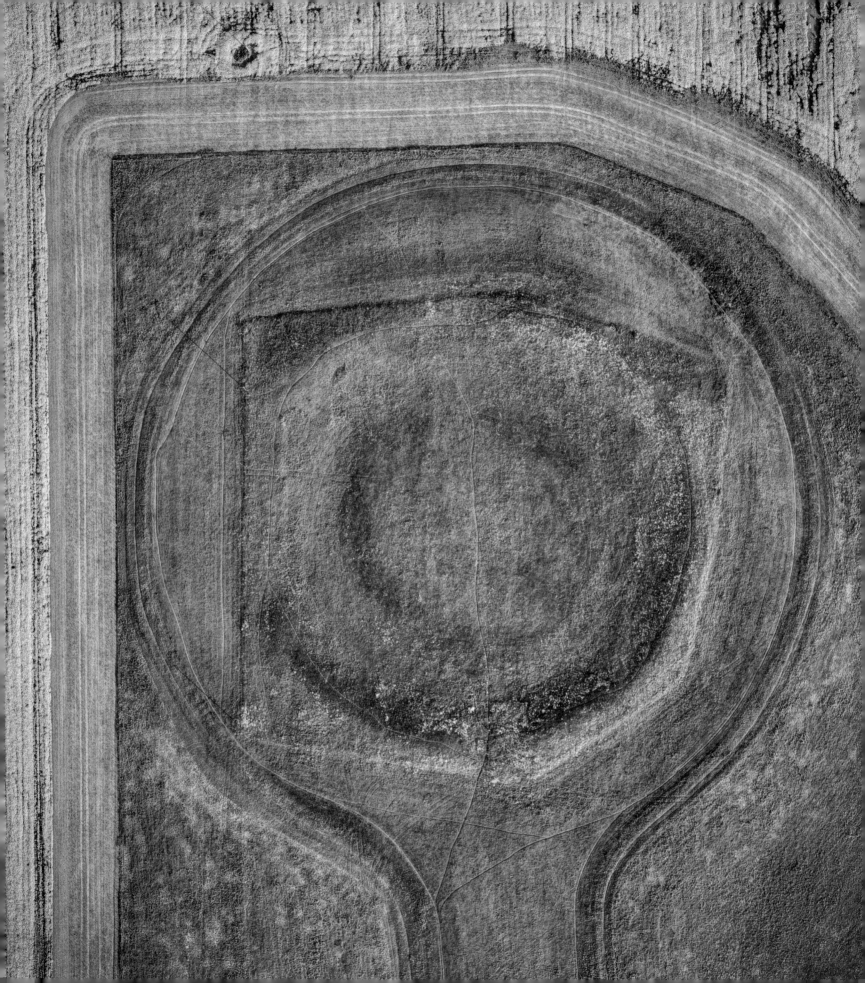

Thornborough Henges North Yorkshire

The largest henge complex between Salisbury Plain and the Orkneys, Thornborough lies close to the banks of the River Ure in Yorkshire. In the Late Neolithic era, three great earth circles, measuring 240 metres (787 feet) in diameter, were carved from this alluvial plain, where a layer of white, crystalline gypsum lies close to the surface. Archaeological excavations suggest the banks and ditches of at least one of them were probably encrusted with the stone, lending a brilliant white appearance that would have sparkled in the sunlight and made the henges stand out in the landscape. Traces of processional avenues lined with timber palisades have also been discovered.

The earthworks were aligned northwest–southeast with the winter solstice sunrise. A pronounced kink in the line mirrors the constellation of Orion's Belt, which has led some to speculate that the Devil's Arrows megaliths, a few miles further southeast along the same axis, may have corresponded to the Pleiades. Of the three, the north circle, these days covered in trees, is the best preserved.

The Tarmac company, which owns the land at Thornborough, has for decades been trying to intensify gravel extraction in the fields adjacent to the henges. Opponents claim quarrying would cause irrevocable damage to the wider ceremonial landscape, which began with the creation in the Middle Neolithic (3500–3300 BC) of a mile-long cursus monument and includes around a dozen different tombs, standing stones and earthworks, most of which have been damaged or completely destroyed.

Priddy Rings Mendip Hills, Somerset

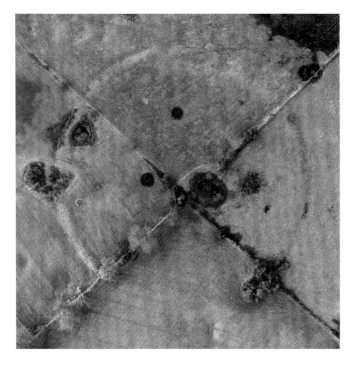

Another henge monument under threat from contemporary land use is the Priddy Ring complex in the Mendip Hills of Somerset. The site actually comprises four circles, ranging from 185 to 194 metres (607 to 636 feet) in diameter. Three are laid out on a single axis, while a fourth, further north and seemingly detached from the others, is a little out of kilter and now virtually invisible.

A Roman road, following the line of an ancient trackway that is believed to have been in use as far back as the Mesolithic era, scythes through this gap (connecting the old lead mines at Charterhouse with the ports at Sea Mills in the Avon Gorge and Uphill near Weston-super-Mare, where the lead was loaded on to ships for export).

Some debate surrounds these enigmatic circles on the Mendip Plateau, which are not henges in the strictest sense (because their ditches lie outside their banks). Archaeological work, however, has shown they were carefully constructed, with inner cores of stone piled between fences of wooden hurdles and posts, which suggests the earthworks were probably more than mere livestock enclosures.

Radiocarbon dating of organic material found at the bottom of the ditches has placed the rings at around 3000 BC, which makes them roughly contemporary with the first Stonehenge circle. Quite why four were created so close together is less certain, but the choice of location, in a natural amphitheatre surrounded by low hills, would seem to be connected to the presence among them of numerous 'swallet holes', or 'dolines' – cavities eroded in the limestone bedrock by rain. The acidic water percolates downwards through invisible cave systems, eventually joining the subterranean river that flows beneath nearby Cheddar Gorge.

There can be little doubt our Neolithic ancestors were aware of this topographical connection, and that they must have been fascinated by the mysterious holes, which have yielded evidence of sacrificial offerings as well as the bones of long-extinct animals, including lynx, rhino and mammoth, which we know were hunted in the interglacial and later Mesolithic periods by inhabitants of the caves at nearby Cheddar Gorge and Burrington Combe (see pp. 26 and 29).

Evidence the area remained a sacred site for thousands of years is to be seen on the ridges to the south of the rings, where Early Bronze Age herders erected two striking linear barrow cemeteries, facing each other across a boggy hollow. Despite being classed as 'scheduled ancient monuments', the Priddy Circles have sustained damage over the years, most recently in 2011 when a local landowner bulldozed a section of Circle No. 1 to make room for a motocross course.

Access to the site is prohibited today, but, in truth, there's little to see at ground level. The grandeur of this extraordinary piece of ancient land art can only be fully appreciated from the air.

The Devil's Quoits Windrush Valley, Oxfordshire

Rubbish tips, industrial estates and flooded gravel pits are not the kind of setting in which you would normally expect to find a Late Neolithic henge. But then, the Devil's Quoits in Oxfordshire is no ordinary ancient monument.

The site, one of a string of large-scale installations built in the Windrush Valley around 2900–2600 BC, was bulldozed by the Royal Air Force in 1940 to make way for a runway, and later quarried for aggregate. Between 2002 and 2008, however, its curves rose from the ashes when the waste management company that owns the land got together with archaeologists from Oxford University to build a replica of the lost structure.

Careful excavation revealed the extent and form of the original henge, along with half a dozen of the megaliths added during the Bronze Age to create a 72-metre (236-foot) wide stone circle. The team decided to recreate the site as it might have looked in the Roman era, so although its ditches and banks are half the size of the originals, they still look 'fresher' than what we're used to seeing elsewhere, which makes for more dramatic shadows and contours; and the knobbly, red-tinged megaliths themselves retain considerable presence.

The approach, via a swathe of landfill and recycling centres, is far from auspicious. But on a winter's morning, the sight of the stones caked in frost with the sun rising from behind a phalanx of misty poplar trees gives some impression of the powerful impact this site would have made in its original incarnation, four thousand or more years ago.

Avebury Henge Wiltshire

Although often dubbed 'Britain's second-largest stone circle', Avebury is a much larger monument than Stonehenge (see p. 110), if you take into account the size of its earthworks. Originally towering 8 metres (26 feet) from the bottom of the ditch to the top of its encircling bank, with a diameter of 347 metres (1,138 feet) at its widest point, the Great Henge was among the most ambitious construction project undertaken by our Neolithic ancestors in Europe.

So-called 'mega henges' began to appear in the landscape towards the end of the fourth millennium BC, providing venues for religious ceremonies held on auspicious days of the solar calendar. These winter and summer solstice gatherings had been a feature of life for centuries, but an intensification of farming and concomitant surge in population resulted in a growth in their scale. Analysis of animal bones (presumed to have been deposited after feasting) also suggests that people travelled to these events over considerable distances – at least as far away as West Wales, and possibly even the Orkney Islands.

The creation of Avebury henge and the circles of huge sarsen stones inside it, a century or two before work began on the enclosure of trilithons at Stonehenge, would have been the marvel of its era. Nearly one hundred megaliths weighing up to 40 tonnes were dragged from the tops of the Marlborough Downs and installed at Avebury, on a platform of level ground close to the source of the River Kennet.

The fact that all this happened indicates a degree of social organization far surpassing that required to create a cursus or chambered tomb: sufficient surplus food to feed an army of diggers had to be stockpiled; tools made from red deer antlers and sheep's shoulder blades; large teams of labourers assembled to prise the sarsens out of the ground, and haul them on specially constructed sleds using long leather ropes; and timber frames and levers prepared to place the megaliths in their sockets.

Ritual specialists and architects will have carefully selected the stones, surveyed the ground and indicated the precise spots where they were to be erected. Over the centuries, the complex was added to and an extensive ceremonial landscape created, featuring two long avenues lined by standing stones that led to the henge from opposing directions.

The precise nature of the rituals performed at Avebury remains a matter of conjecture. Modern New Age theories assert the henge was a meeting point of male and female 'energy lines', while archaeologists tend to interpret the site as evidence for the emergence of a hierarchical society dominated by a chiefly elite. Whatever the original symbolic or political significance of the monument, it was one whose heyday through the third millennium BC spanned an era of massive cultural change.

Stonehenge Wiltshire

Avebury may be bigger and Brodgar set amid lovelier scenery, but the sheer monumentality of Stonehenge inspires awe like no other Neolithic site in Britain.

The circle as it appears today was the culmination of a sequence of construction projects beginning with a scattering of chambered tombs in the early fourth millennium BC. These were followed by the Lesser and Greater Cursus earthworks (see p. 50) and, around 3100–3000 BC, a circular ditch-and-bank enclosure 110 metres (360 feet) wide, in which a collection of large bluestones brought from the Preseli Hills of West Wales was first erected. Various configurations of timber posts and rearrangements of the bluestones then gave way, around 2500 BC, to a circle of sixty enormous sarsen megaliths, quarried on the Marlborough Downs 25 kilometres (16 miles) north.

The sarsens were dressed in situ and capped with giant lintels held together by a combination of tongue-and-groove and mortise-and-tenon joints. Inside this was placed a horseshoe of fifteen even larger orthostats, towering 7 metres (23 feet) above ground (from sockets 2.4 metres or 8 feet deep) – the famous 'trilithons' that have come to define the monument in the popular imagination.

The mystery of why our Neolithic ancestors chose what at first glance appears a rather nondescript location on Salisbury Plain was explained when researchers conducting geophysical tests in the area discovered a tract of chalk bedrock scoured by long grooves. Formed by running water at the end of the Holocene, these align perfectly with the summer solstice sunset – a phenomenon that seems to have been noticed by Mesolithic hunter-gatherers, who erected a cluster of tall timber posts on the site.

Archaeological research has revealed how, during the later Neolithic period, Stonehenge served primarily as a focus for funerary rites. Participants are believed to have congregated at nearby Durrington (see p. 114) before proceeding a couple of miles downstream to a landing stage marked by a small circle of bluestones. From there, worshippers would follow a ceremonial walkway, known today as the 'Avenue', over a ridge and down the other side across a dry combe, before ascending to the great henge.

Although invisible at ground level today, traces of the Avenue are still clearly discernible from the air, underlining how the great stone circle stood as the pivotal point in a wider ceremonial landscape, demarcated by long palisades of timber posts and processional paths of compacted chalk.

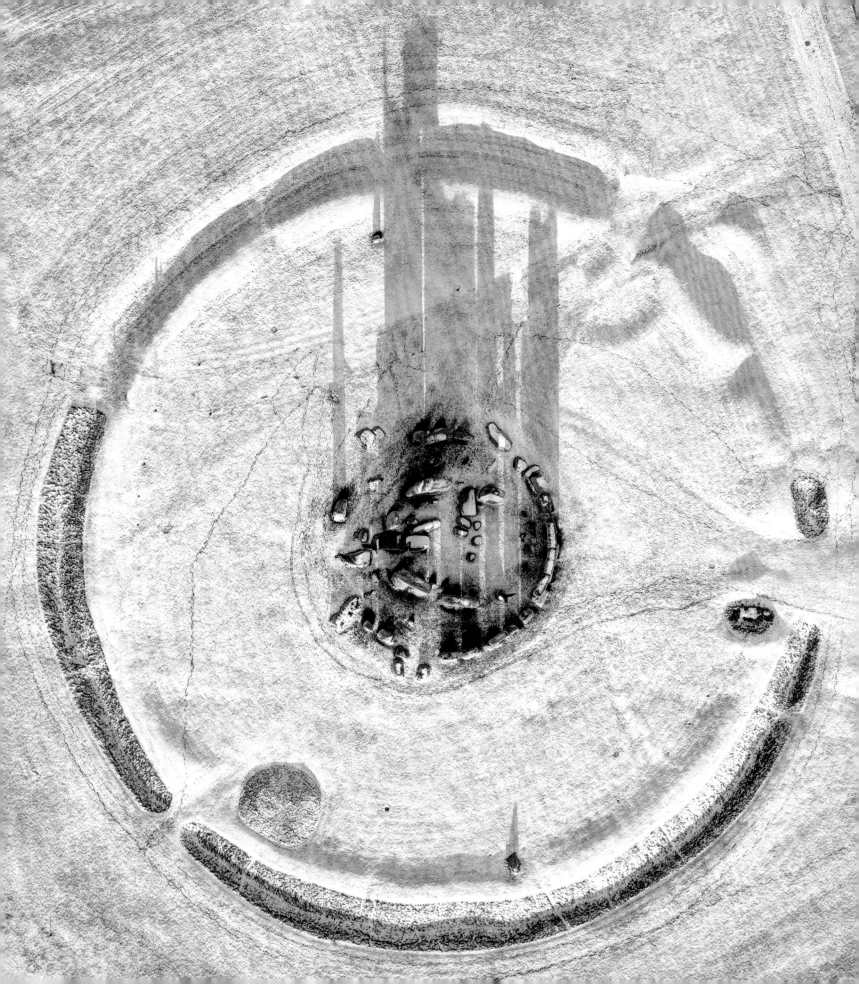

Durrington Walls Wiltshire

'Mega henges' – giant ditch-and-bank enclosures – were a defining feature of the landscape of Late Neolithic Britain. Although not strictly a henge and greatly diminished by millennia of ploughing and erosion, this huge earthwork on Salisbury Plain has nevertheless been the subject of considerable archaeological scrutiny thanks to its proximity to Stonehenge, a couple of miles to the west.

A rescue dig conducted in 1967 to 1968 ahead of road construction proved the Neolithic origins of the site, which sits on sloping land above the Wiltshire Avon (visible on the far left of the image). A wealth of pottery came to light in the course of the dig, though considerably fewer everyday tools (such as flint scrapers for cleaning hides) than was the norm. Instead, the archaeologists discovered numerous finely made bone pins for securing clothing and hair, alongside evidence of large-scale feasting, in the form of pits containing vast middens of animal bones and Grooved Ware pots. Clearly, Durrington Walls was less of a workaday agricultural centre than one with ceremonial underpinnings.

This hypothesis has been borne out by the many high-profile digs carried out here since, in which the hard, chalk-plaster floors of many square and rectangular Neolithic houses have been discovered, spanning a period of around three centuries from 2600 BC.

Punctuated by four openings, the enormous ditch-and-bank 'walls' around the site date from 2480 to 2460 BC – Durrington's peak period – when this is believed to have been the largest settlement in northern Europe, accommodating four or five thousand people. The earthworks were constructed in twenty-two segments by gangs of around two hundred labourers. Whether a small number of gangs worked their way sequentially around the site, or a couple of dozen separate teams toiled at the same time in one big push is not known.

The space inside the ramparts was divided into four distinct quadrants, holding around 250 houses each on terraces levelled with turf stacks. A clearing in the centre revolved around a larger, special building set in its own compound, flanked to its east and north by two large, concentric rings of timber posts, aligned with the winter solstice sunrise.

The population of Durrington would probably have been seasonal, swelling around the times of the winter and summer solstices, when travellers from across southern Britain may have converged here to feast and perform rituals. Those arriving by river would have entered the enclave via a 15-metre (49-foot) wide chalk-lined 'avenue', also orientated on the solstitial axis and flanked by low banks of compacted earth.

Woodhenge Durrington, Wiltshire

On a cloudless morning in 1925, Squadron Leader Gilbert Insall – an early pioneer of aerial archaeology – was flying over Salisbury Plain when he noticed a cluster of enigmatic crop marks in a field immediately south of Durrington Walls. The photograph he took of the site clearly showed six concentric rings of dark spots in the ripening wheat below, some of them very substantial, alongside a cluster of other faint circles to the south.

The image inspired local archaeologist Maud Cunnington and her husband, Ben, to begin excavation work the following year. Their dig revealed a total of 168 holes, forming an oval shape 40 metres (131 feet) across at its widest point. The largest were around 2 metres (6½ feet) deep – sizeable enough to hold a post 7.5 metres (25 feet) tall, weighing 5 tonnes. The remains of earth ramps showed how these giant timbers were heaved into position.

An earthwork enclosure surrounded the monument, entered via a gap to the northeast aligned with the summer solstice sunrise. Dug midway through the third millennium BC, at around the same time as the 'walls' of the adjacent Neolithic settlement, the ditch-and-bank enclosure is similar in size and orientation to nearby Stonehenge (see p. 110), which inspired the Cunningtons to christen the site 'Woodhenge'.

Various theories have been advanced for how the henge, and its siblings inside the main Durrington enclosure, may have been used, but it now seems likely they did not support roofs and were open to the sky.

Archaeologist Mike Parker Pearson has famously suggested that the emphasis on perishable wood, as opposed to permanent stone, points to Durrington being some kind of symbolic 'Domain of the Living', where feasting took place as part of solstitial rituals. Connected via the River Avon, which flows through the valley below, Stonehenge would have been the opposing 'Domain of the Ancestors' associated with funerary rites.

Could this juxtaposition, and the ceremonial journey between the two sites, have represented the transition from life to death? The connection of the two by means of the river and processional chalk avenues certainly lends credence to the idea, as does the existence of similar ritual dichotomies in the anthropological record, including a traditional society in Madagascar who continued to build megalithic structures within living memory.

After completing the 1926 dig, the Cunningtons marked the holes they had excavated with concrete posts, which survive to this day. The evocative shadows they cast at dawn conjure the ghostly presence of their Neolithic predecessors when viewed from directly above.

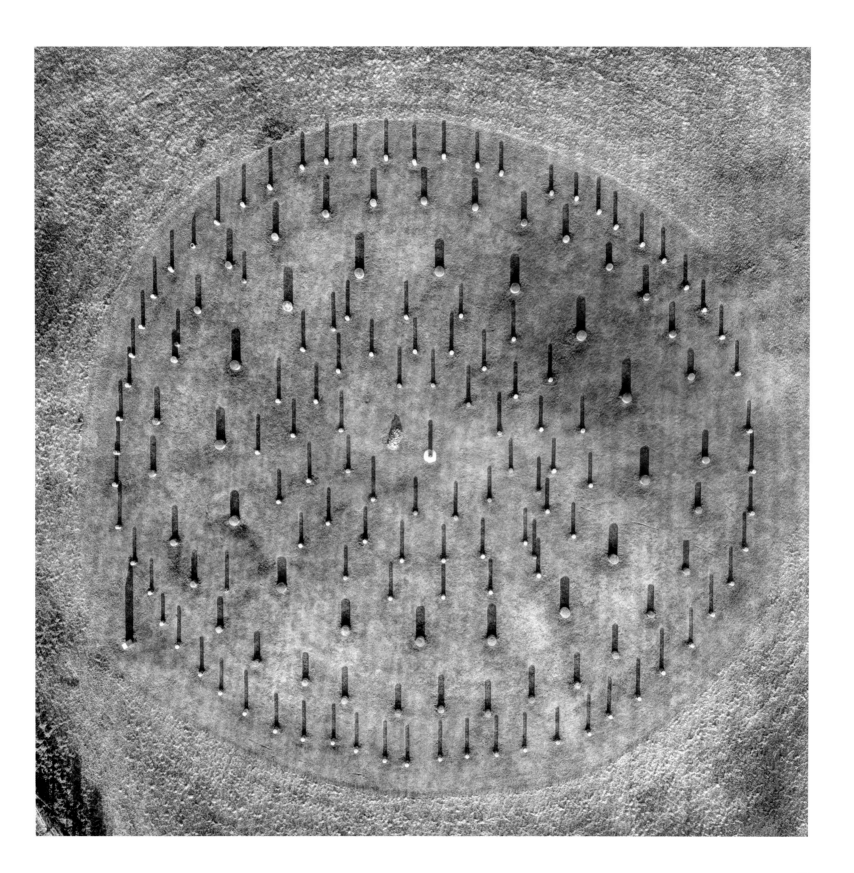

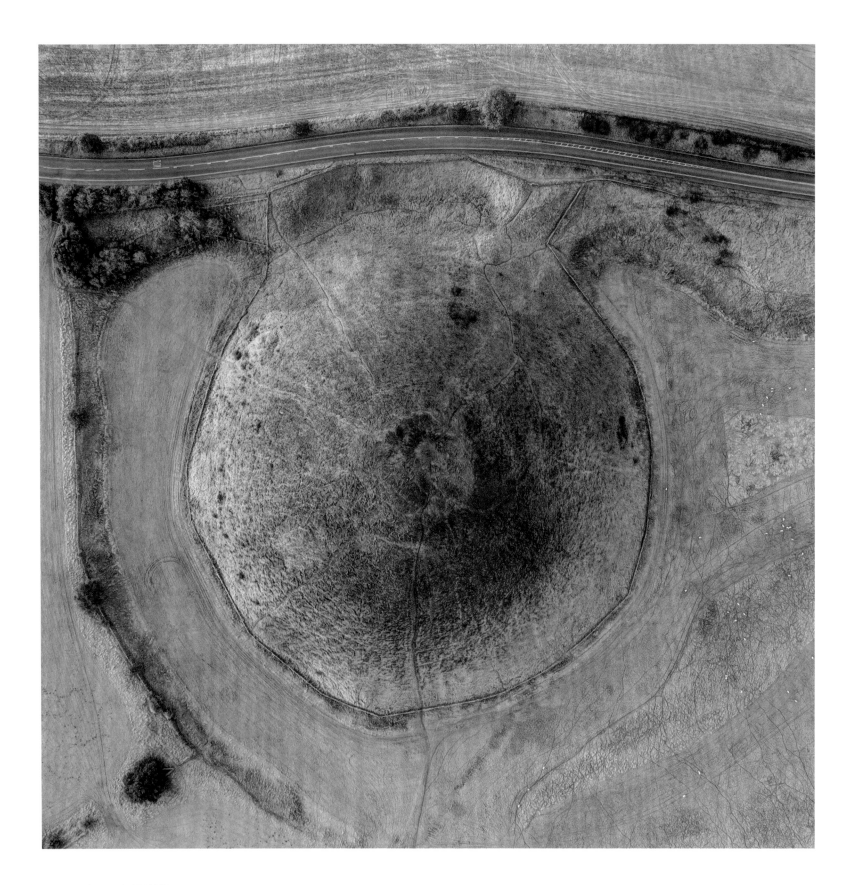

Silbury Hill Wiltshire

One of the great enigmas of British prehistory rises from a boggy field just south of Avebury, close to the head of the River Kennet in Wiltshire. An imposing 40 metres (130 feet) from head to toe, Silbury Hill is by far the largest man-made mound surviving from the Neolithic period in Europe, and a wonder of ancient engineering. It was constructed in phases between 2700 and 2300 BC, starting with a heap of compacted gravel and gradually growing in scale as successive layers of chalk and clay were added. Although simple in outline, its inner structure, based around a circular kerb of sarsen boulders dragged from the surrounding uplands, was sophisticated. It has been estimated that five hundred men would have taken fifteen years to complete the project – a gargantuan enterprise even by the standards of the area, hinting at the existence of a chiefly elite and powerful belief system capable of co-opting and resourcing a large workforce over a sustained period of time.

Generations of antiquarians and archaeologists have probed, scraped and tunnelled into the eminence, but little of note has been found beyond the discovery at its base of winged ants (proving work on Silbury began in late summer), a handful of animal bones and fragments of antler picks.

Some clue as to its symbolic significance may lie in its proximity to important springs, whose waters flowed around the bottom of the hill. In its heyday, Silbury would have been surrounded by a shallow moat (from which building material was obtained), and for much of the winter the hill still rises from flooded pasture, creating a dramatic spectacle for travellers passing on the adjacent A4 highway.

Much speculation surrounds its original function. Avebury Henge (see p. 106) and West Kennet Long Barrow (see p. 41) are both visible from the summit, suggesting Silbury formed a part of the ceremonial circuit followed on foot by visiting worshippers. Others, inspired by the theories of author Michael Dames, claim the mound represented the belly of a giant, pregnant fertility goddess. The fact that the Romans established an important shrine to Ceres, goddess of fertility, nearby – a waystage on the old road from London to Bath – is given as evidence to support this theory. But the theory's detractors rightly point out that the different parts of the wider 'body' of the 'goddess' were constructed several centuries apart and could not therefore have formed part of an overarching plan.

Whatever its intended use, Silbury was the last great ritual building project undertaken on the chalklands of Neolithic Wessex. Some have interpreted its awe-inspiring scale as a response to the appearance in the region of the first Beaker people. Whether the focus of a fertility cult, a stone-age 'axis mundi' or an assertion of regional identity, the mound was a potent final flowering of a culture on the brink of massive change.

The Copper and Bronze Ages

By around 2500 BC (in the Late Neolithic period, during which the great circle of trilithons at Stonehenge was erected), the landscape of Britain had been radically transformed by the arrival of herder-farmers from northern France. Population was on the increase and larger, dynamic communities were coming together to create monumental henges and stone circles, where they gathered in numbers to feast and celebrate festivals coinciding with key phases in the solar and lunar calendars.

Distinct regional cultures had coalesced around these monuments, distinguished in the archaeological record primarily by styles of pottery. At the same time, a striking degree of cultural conformity is apparent in this era. Ideas, beliefs and ritual practices were clearly shared over long distances, following both maritime and land routes between large henges and other ceremonial centres.

Recounted by storytellers around hearths the length and breadth of these islands, foundation myths and beliefs in the powers of such sites must have underpinned annual festivals, where ceremonial gatherings would have taken place, perhaps in parallel with livestock fairs. Polished stone axes may have changed hands at such events, along with other valuable commodities. Marriages too could have been brokered, and connections between lineages or distant populations cemented by gift exchange.

One can never know for sure exactly what type of interactions took place. But it is safe to assume they did, and that there must have been considerable movement of people around Britain. Moreover, we know from items unearthed in Late Neolithic contexts that these travel networks extended far beyond British shores, connecting communities in the Hebrides, Ireland, the Paris Basin, Rhineland and Brittany, and even further afield in Iberia, the Alps and the Mediterranean.

It was via these routes that a new, and hugely influential, traveller began to appear in Britain around 2500 BC.

The Beaker Phenomenon

Named after the distinctively decorated terracotta pots frequently found in their graves, the 'Beaker Folk' began to arrive in Britain in the mid- to late third millennium BC. Originating in continental Europe, they were harbingers of a technological revolution rooted in metalworking, knowledge of which the incomers are believed to have introduced to these islands, along with a package of new cultural practices.

Yar Tor, Dartmoor

Genomic research has tended to favour the latter scenario. Much work remains to be done on the subject, but the gist of the latest genetic discoveries is that a rapid turnover in population occurred after 2500 BC: the dark-skinned, dark-haired, southern European-looking Britons of the Neolithic era yielded almost completely to the paler-skinned, lighter-haired migrants. While in continental Europe the Beaker people gradually blended with the populations they encountered, in Britain they supplanted their predecessors in a surprisingly short period of around three centuries. By 2000 BC, 90 per cent of the genes of the British population appear to have had 'Steppe ancestry', pointing to origins in the distant Pontic-Caspian region, from where the nomadic-pastoralist ancestors of the Beaker people first migrated westwards centuries earlier, travelling on ox-drawn wagons with horses and domesticated animals.

It is less clear why these newcomers appeared in Britain in the first place. The most plausible explanation is that their arrival may have been propelled by the search, via existing trade routes across Europe and along the Atlantic coast, for new sources of copper ore.

Barrows and Cemeteries

Varying in scale and shape, Early Bronze Age barrows are typically classified by archaeologists into five main types – bowl, bell, disc, saucer and pond – defined by their forms and surrounding ditches or inner platforms. Some didn't contain any burials, while others held the remains of multiple individuals spanning centuries of use. In upland areas, they tended to be cairns made of dry stones, sometimes encircled by kerbs or surmounted by platforms.

Although barrows sometimes occur in clusters of a dozen or so, they are often interpreted as evidence for the emergence in Britain of a less communal way of life, stressing the primacy of personhood and immediate family rather than the wider clan, as was the case with the large chambered tombs of previous eras.

Clues to their wider significance may also be found in the choice of locations. Larger barrow cemeteries often crop up close to rivers, springs and confluences, while some of the country's biggest mounds are to be found on prominent peaks, scarps or watersheds. The latter might hint at the existence of some kind of hierarchy, as if the high-status individuals to whom the graves belonged dominated the wider territories encompassed by the views from them. Sight lines between barrows and cemeteries are also perhaps indicative of the way landscape may have been divided up between lineages.

The most visible impact of their presence from an archaeological perspective was on the wider landscape, which became studded with round earth mounds marking the sites of burials. Representing a radical break with the traditions of the indigenous Neolithic population (who by this time practised mainly cremation or other means of disposing of bodies that left no trace), these 'barrows' were expressions of a culture whose roots stretched back over several centuries to the fringes of Europe.

The Beaker phenomenon had two distinct origin strands: one in the plains of eastern Europe and another in the Iberian Peninsula, where the oldest Beaker graves found on the Continent have been unearthed. Pressing west and northwards respectively, these two migration waves met and intermingled in an area extending from the Paris Basin to the Rhineland and what we now call the Low Countries in the twenty-eighth and twenty-seventh centuries, and it was from here that the first Beaker people travelled to Britain.

The nature of the relations between the incomers and their indigenous hosts remains a matter of conjecture. While some assert that the Beaker Folk were few in number and that their burial practices (and presumably religious beliefs) were taken up in a process of diffusion by the locals, others argue that the influx must have been on a large scale to have made the impact it did.

A Chalcolithic Elite

Some of the richest Beaker burials discovered in Britain lie in the immediate vicinity of Stonehenge – the most impressive monument in Europe during what archaeologists refer to as the 'Chalcolithic', or 'Copper Age'. Early Beaker burial mounds also feature in the ceremonial landscapes of Avebury and numerous other Late Neolithic sites, suggesting not only that the newcomers must have participated in rituals at the same ceremonial centres as the indigenous population, but also that their presence at them was welcome.

It is tempting to imagine how the locals might have responded to the arrival of these handsomely dressed visitors, with their gleaming copper daggers, amber necklaces and gold jewelry. Such luxuries, and the knowledge of how to obtain or create them, must have seemed miraculous. We know from graves such as that of the Amesbury Archer, found in a site near Stonehenge, and his close relative nearby (believed to be a cousin, who grew up in Britain) that Beaker incomers settled and had children.

Isotopic analysis has also revealed that a large proportion of them died many miles from their place of birth, and that they spent much of their lives on the move (this might in part explain why so few houses and permanent settlements from the era have come to light). The inference is that our Early Bronze Age ancestors, like their Neolithic predecessors, led a predominantly transhumant existence: following herds of livestock between seasonal pastures.

Rich burials such as those around Stonehenge also point to the existence of some kind of elite capable of acquiring exotic commodities from other regions and overseas (principally black jet from Whitby, amber from the Baltic and Irish gold). This elite must have dominated maritime trade, which intensified considerably with the advent of bronze towards the end of the third millennium.

The Magical Alloy

Knowledge of bronze casting had already become widespread in Europe by the time it reached Britain and the required ingredients were in great demand among the Minoans, Mycenaeans and other sophisticated city states trading around the Mediterranean. Tin in particular was rare in continental Europe and its discovery in the far west of Cornwall led to the development of an important seaborne trade towards the end of the third millennium BC.

Herder-farmers in West Penwith gathered ore exposed by cliff erosion and washed down moorland rivers and smelted it into round ingots, which they then transported overland and by boat down the Tamar, possibly to Mount Batten – a *presqu'île* in Plymouth harbour to which traders from Brittany and Normandy travelled each summer. They, in turn, would carry the metal south across Biscay to Galicia, from where Iberian merchants would ferry it onwards via the Tagus Estuary to the Phoenician ports in the Mediterranean. The same routes would doubtless have been used to export Welsh copper from Anglesey and Great Orme near Llandudno in later centuries.

The rarity of ore may explain why bronze was taken up relatively slowly on the Continent. In Britain, by contrast, where tin and copper were more readily procured, it was embraced rapidly and completely.

Within a century of its arrival, bronze was being cast into a variety of desirable objects by British smiths – initially flat daggers, axes and halberds (a two-headed poleaxe) and later spears, palstaves, rapiers and socket axes – which were widely exported across northern Europe.

Bronze axes enabled dramatic improvements in boat building. Vessels made of oak planks, stitched together with yew lashings and caulked with sap and pig fat, made long-distance maritime trade more practicable and lucrative.

Several examples of Bronze Age boats have come to light in Britain, the best preserved of them discovered during a road construction project near Dover in 1992. The 'Dover Boat' has been dated by dendrochronologists to 1575–1520 BC, by which time the old Atlantic sea routes had been eclipsed by crossings from what is now the Netherlands and Belgium to the Thames and southern North Sea ports.

Merchants and Feasts

As well as being evidence of cross-Channel trade in southeast England, the Dover Boat also points to the emergence of a new mercantile class. No longer were the luxuries glinting in early Beaker burials – or the means of acquiring them – the unique preserve of a chiefly elite. With the development of bronze tools in the first half of the second

Kilmartin Glen, Argyll

123

millennium BC, many more ocean-going vessels were making the journey to Europe and the old luxuries somewhat lost their cachet. Wealthy graves brimming with treasure slowly fell out of fashion, to be replaced by cremation burials in flat cemeteries. The elite lineages, meanwhile, embraced other ways of demonstrating their prestige and affluence.

One of them – the tradition of feasting – originated in continental Europe and travelled to Britain on the back of the Middle to Late Bronze Age trade boom. Weighty cauldrons, flesh hooks, roasting spits and situlas (deep bronze buckets) start to appear around this time. Feasts would have been held in large roundhouses, probably around open hearths with the cauldrons hanging from the roof apex and the guests seated around them in circles, the most senior and important in the front and their entourage behind. Beer made from malted grain and flavoured with herbs and honey, and possibly laced with intoxicants such as cannabis, would have been consumed.

The Bronze Age Watershed: 1500 BC

The middle of the second millennium BC saw a number of other significant developments in Britain, foremost among them a shift in patterns of land use. Human-made boundaries forming coaxial field systems and linear trenches bordering more extensive ranches began to appear in the landscape for the first time, implying an intensification of both agriculture and, by inference, of the coercive power of the elites. The conclusion must be that control over the land and its produce began replacing control over trade in exotic substances as the dominant motivating force in society.

In order to provide feasts, the Bronze Age elite of Britain needed to generate ever greater surpluses, which some archaeologists believe they most likely achieved by subdividing plots and leasing them (along with livestock) to farmers in exchange for a percentage share of the harvest. Concurrent with the advent of land enclosure is the creation of substantial homesteads and ring forts in which the surpluses could be stored and protected.

Beautifully made bronze rapiers and shields were other ways this elite displayed their wealth and power. The Late Bronze Age sees a dramatic proliferation in the variety and number of such items. Different styles of swords emerged in different regions, forming clusters by means of which archaeologists have been able to discern regional groups and trade connections between population centres extending across Europe.

Climate Change: 1000 BC

Towards the end of the second millennium BC, the British climate took a marked downturn, growing cooler, wetter and stormier. While the southern chalklands remained relatively unaffected, populous upland areas such as Dartmoor and Bodmin – where large settlements of herders produced meat, cheese and hides – were deserted. Blanket bogs of peat and moss formed, destroying the grasslands forever.

Sometime between 1155 and 1141 BC, the eruption of a volcano in Iceland also had a dramatic impact on the weather in the far north of Scotland. Ash clouds led to much colder conditions, crop failures and, most likely, famine.

Genomic research conducted on Late Bronze Age skeletons across Britain has also revealed that the period from 1400 to 870 BC saw a significant influx of migrants from continental Europe. It is estimated that around half of the ancestry of later Britons derives from this migration wave. No one has yet come up with a convincing theory to account for it, but the phenomenon coincides with the patterns of land use described above, as well as shifts in ritual practices.

Giving Back to the Gods

One of the most significant shifts, from the point of view of the archaeological record, is the custom of depositing metal items in lakes, rivers and bogs. No one can say for sure what the thinking was behind these ritual depositions. But they were common across Britain and often extraordinary in scale.

At Flag Fen, near Peterborough in East Anglia, a vast array of bronze objects (including swords, socket axes, spearheads and items of jewelry) were placed in fenland accessed via piers or boardwalks built of 60,000 oak timbers. At Llyn y Fan Fawr, in the Brecon Beacons of South Wales, artefacts of the highest quality were discovered in the acidic peat bed of a mountain lake. Among them were a magnificent cauldron weighing over 7.5 kilograms (16½ pounds), horse harnesses, sickles and chisels, along with some of the earliest iron objects found in Britain, where they were deposited at the very end of the Bronze Age. On the northern bank of the Thames in London, some 453 bronze spearheads and adzes were deliberately consigned to the silt, seemingly at the same time, around 900 BC.

Patterns have been discerned in these and other metal offerings around the country. It seems as if different types of objects were deposited in different contexts: swords and spears in flowing rivers (notably the Thames and the Trent), everyday metal items and jewelry in lakes, bogs and fens.

Numerous explanations have been advanced for this phenomenon. The weapons may have belonged to defeated enemies or to warriors whose cremated remains had been disposed of at the same place, or perhaps treasured possessions were left in order to petition the deities residing in the water. Many archaeologists believe bronze was regarded as a material deriving from the gods, and which had to be returned to them eventually.

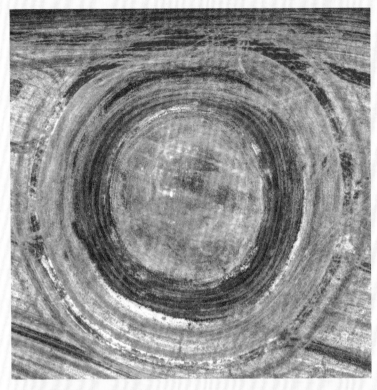

Roundway Hill, Devizes, Wiltshire

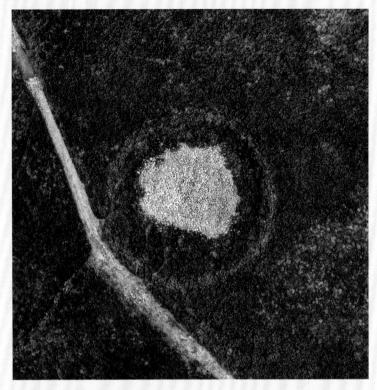

Rowbarrow, Codsend Moor, Exmoor

Corndon Down, Dartmoor

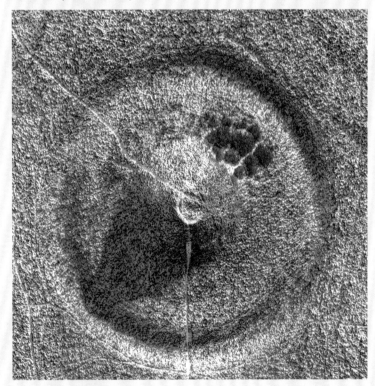

Cursus Barrows, Wiltshire

Normanton Barrow Cemetery Wiltshire

That Stonehenge (see p. 110) and its wider ceremonial landscape attracted visitors from afar at the very dawn of the Chalcolithic, or Copper Age, we know from the wealth of Beaker graves discovered in the area (among them that of the Amesbury Archer, see p. 123). The majority were dug out of the chalk bedrock and surmounted by circular mounds of earth gathered from a surrounding ditch. Although many of these early Beaker-period tumuli had eroded away or been ploughed flat by the early nineteenth century, enough survived to yield a rough chronology.

Dating from the end of the third millennium, the first were grouped mainly to the west of Stonehenge in plots close to the Greater Cursus (see p. 50) and Early Neolithic long barrows. In later centuries, however, an array of larger tumuli and more elaborate 'fancy barrows' began to appear along a ridge immediately south of the stone circle.

Objects unearthed in the cemetery include a couple of rare bone whistles or flutes: one fashioned from the hollowed-out tibia of a crane, and the other from a human femur. Judging from the wealth of grave goods discovered here on Normanton Down, this must have been sacred ground set aside exclusively for the Wessex elite. A marked absence of flint scatters suggests everyday activities were excluded, though whether religious ceremonies took place here it is impossible to say.

Today, despite its proximity to Stonehenge, the Normanton cemetery is little visited. Glimpsed fleetingly from cars passing on the nearby A303, the barrows are the domain of grazing bullocks and, in early March when hard frosts frequently encrust the grasslands of Salisbury Plain, pairs of boxing hares.

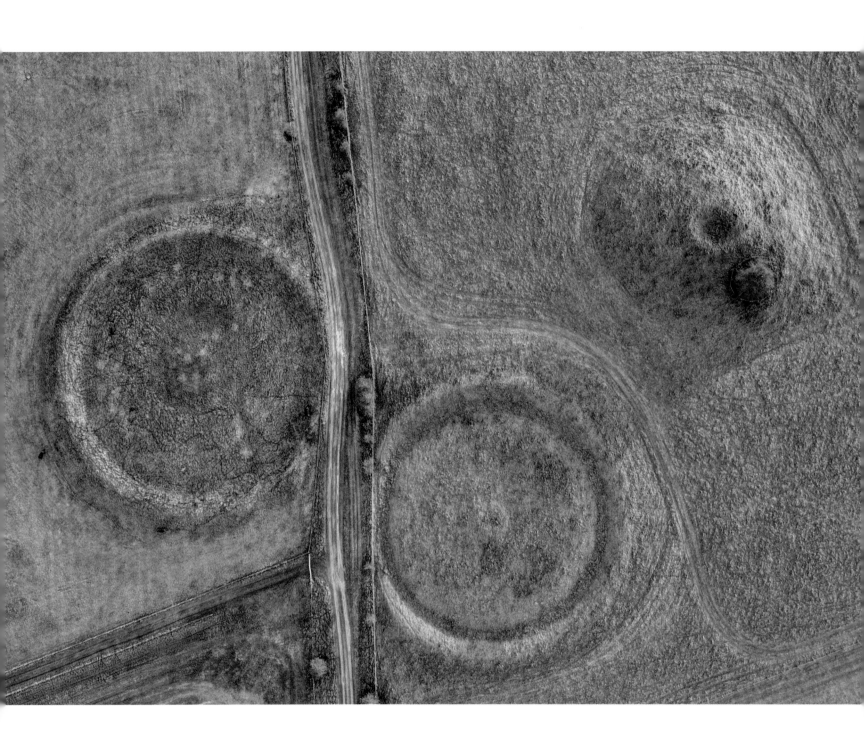

The Bush Barrow Normanton Down, Wiltshire

In September 1808, a wool merchant from Heytesbury in Wiltshire named William Cunnington arrived in a pony and trap on Salisbury Plain. Accompanied by his trusty labourers, Stephen and John Parker, he was on a mission to excavate barrows in the Stonehenge area. Cunnington was finically supported in his endeavours by a wealthy heir to a banking dynasty, Sir Richard Colt-Hoare, from the Stourhead Estate near Mere. The pair had teamed up four years earlier and would, over two decades, disembowel around three hundred Bronze Age burial mounds in their home county, amassing in the process a vast hoard of artefacts.

One barrow in particular had attracted Cunnington's attention: a large, round and seemingly unpromising heap overgrown with 'furze and heath'. Part of the cemetery on Normanton Down, the 'Bush Barrow' had resisted his efforts once before. But on the second attempt, he and his team literally struck gold.

Arrayed around the crouched skeleton of a large male discovered at ground level was a bewildering jigsaw puzzle of items that collectively represent one of the richest burials ever discovered from the Early Bronze Age in Europe. They included a beautiful copper dagger from Brittany, its hilt adorned with thousands of tiny gold studs; a polished mace head made from a fossilized sea sponge, and what is believed to have been fragments of bone

marquetry cut into zigzags that would have decorated its shaft. Most exciting of all, though, were the gold treasures, foremost among them an exquisitely decorated belt buckle and a plaque inscribed with geometric patterns.

Known as the 'Bush Barrow Lozenge', the latter would have been worn as a breast plate or pendant. Intriguingly, the angles of its outer edges, along with those of the bands of decoration, were cut at an angle of just under 81 degrees – replicating the angle separating the alignments of the summer and winter solstices at Stonehenge. Whether this identifies the lozenge as a ritual or architectural tool is a moot point, but the prominence of the auspicious angle cannot be coincidental.

More certain is that the occupant of this grave was a person of the highest rank – perhaps a priest or chief. The extraordinary richness of the goods interred with him, and in similar graves across the chalklands, demonstrates the desire on the part of the Wessex elite to outshine their rivals. Such a hoard of precious and exotic materials is pure Bronze Age bling: high-status individuals from diverse regions and lineages would have congregated at Stonehenge for important festivals, and regalia clearly played an important role in the gatherings, reinforcing rank and power.

The Bush Barrow Lozenge, along with the other treasures from the site, is displayed in the Wiltshire Museum, Devizes.

Opthalmologists have claimed that without a magnifying glass, the inscriptions on the famous Bush Barrow Lozenge could only have been done by a twelve-year-old (most likely under the supervision of an older master maker).

Winterbourne Stoke Wiltshire

A few miles southwest of Stonehenge along the busy A303, the village of Winterbourne Stoke is surrounded by low hills whose crests are studded with numerous Early Bronze Age barrow cemeteries.

Two of these, just north of the village, face each other from opposite sides of the pretty Till Valley, overlooking a chalk stream – a view that can have changed little since William Cunnington and his helpers got to work on the mounds in 1809.

Both groups, each comprising a dozen barrows of various sizes, are encircled by low banks believed to have been added in the Saxon era (suggesting they continued to be valued into Medieval times). The outstanding find at the one on the west side of the combe, in an enclosure known as 'the Coniger', was a beautiful and rare composite necklace of long, tapering beads made from porcelain-coloured fossil shells and fired white clay. Shale rings, jet buttons and beaver teeth, as well as numerous Beaker and collared urns, were also unearthed in the area.

Further east, within sight of Stonehenge, is another important group of barrows clustered on the north side of a busy crossroads on the London–Salisbury road. Aligned along a solstitial axis defined by an Early Neolithic long barrow, they include a couple of exceptionally large mounds excavated by Cunnington's crew in 1809.

In one of these, the diggers found a chunk of fossilized wood 'resembling a bunch of twigs'. Beneath it was buried a cist in which a skeleton had been laid to rest in the hollowed-out trunk of an elm tree. One of the longest copper daggers ever unearthed in an Early Bronze Age context also accompanied the occupant of the grave on his journey to the afterlife, along with a bronze pin with an ivory handle and an elegantly shaped spearhead. In honour of this exceptional hoard, Richard Colt-Hoare dubbed the barrow 'the King's Mound'.

A footpath through the adjacent beech coppice leads from a conveniently sited layby on the A303 to the barrows, which are protected by the National Trust.

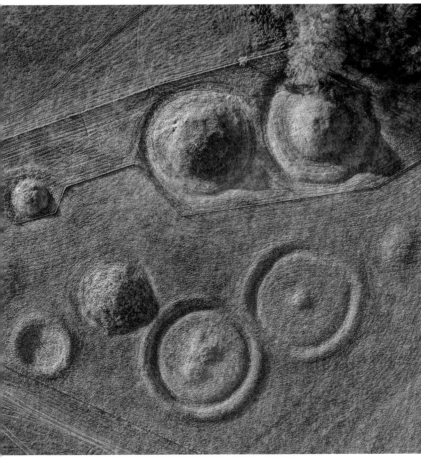
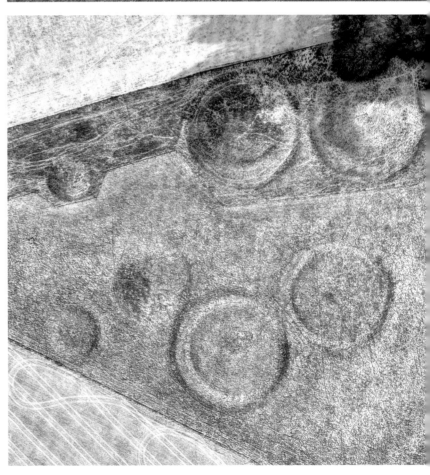

The Cursus Barrows Wiltshire

In a fenced enclosure to the northwest of Stonehenge lies a spectacular row of bell barrows dating from the Early Bronze Age. Although they have an interrupted line of sight to the nearby circle of sarsen trilithons, the placement next to and in alignment with the Greater Cursus (see p. 50) was clearly intentional (the Dorset Cursus on Cranborne Chase also has several groups of barrows from the same period alongside it), showing that even monuments that were much older and had perhaps fallen out of use by the time the first Beaker burials appeared on Salisbury Plain were venerated by the new settlers from the Continent (and their descendants).

The enclosed area shown in the photograph holds half a dozen of the eighteen mounds in this cemetery, dotted along a low rise over a distance of roughly 1.2 kilometres (nearly ¾ mile). Excavations here revealed Beaker and collared urn graves, with both inhumations and cremated remains, and the usual array of exotic commodities favoured by the elite of Early Bronze Age Wessex.

The standout find here was a necklace comprising eighteen large beads of amber and two of glassy-blue faience (a colour combination that, coincidentally, crops up in the coral and turquoise jewelry of the Tibetan Plateau and numerous Native American peoples).

Although amber from the Baltic had been finding its way to Britain for centuries, faience was a relatively new, artificial material that appears to have been a speciality of southern England. It is produced by blending crushed quartz with lime and water, moulding the resulting compound around a straw to create the perforation for a bead, and then adding a glaze of powder of lime, quartz and copper powder (the latter is responsible for the vivid sky-blue hue) before firing. Faience beads believed to have originated in Wessex have been found at sites in Brittany, the Channel Islands and the Netherlands.

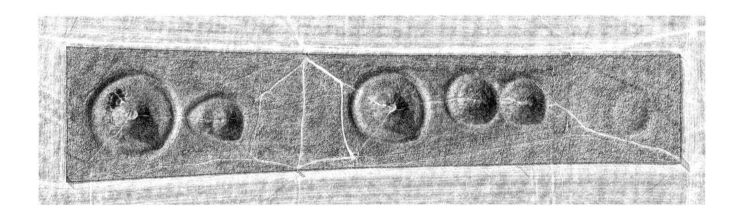

Oakley Down Cranborne Chase, Dorset

Perhaps the most visually arresting of all the Bronze Age cemeteries surviving on the chalklands of Wessex is the one at Oakley Down, on Cranborne Chase in north Dorset. Bounded on one side by the busy Blandford–Salisbury road, and on the other by its Roman equivalent, the Ackling Dyke, the plot includes several types of barrow, many of them built on a large scale. They are believed to have belonged to the inhabitants of a cluster of farmsteads located twenty minutes' walk west across the fields near the village of Sixpenny Handley.

William Cunnington and Richard Colt-Hoare investigated nineteen of the Oakley tumuli, encountering some particularly violent weather when they began to tunnel down into one of the larger mounds. In his book *The History of Ancient Wiltshire*, Colt-Hoare recalled that the excavators had to take refuge inside the hole they had dug after lightning struck their shovel and sent a hail of 'large flints [pouring] down on us from the summit of the barrow so abundantly and so forcibly that we were obliged to quit our hiding place, and abide the pelting of the pitiless storm upon the bleak and unsheltered down'.

Such a bad omen would surely have sent a party more prone to superstition running for their lives. It didn't, but one member of the group, an Anglican priest named William Lisle Bowles, was inspired to write a poem about the event, casting their attempt to break into the grave as a violation – and ultimately a futile one at that:

> *See! Taranis* [the Celtic god of thunder] *descends to save*
> *His hero's violated grave,*
> *And shakes, beneath the lightning's glare,*
> *The sulphur from his blazing hair!*
> *... Hence! yet, though my grave ye spoil,*
> *Dark oblivion marks your toil:*
> *Deep the clouds of ages roll –*
> *History drops her mould'ring scroll –*
> *And never shall reveal the name,*
> *Of Him, who scorns her transient fame.*

Among the plentiful finds unearthed by Cunnington's team (now held in Wiltshire Museum, Devizes) was a pair of terracotta incense cups. Precisely what our Bronze Age ancestors burned in them no one has been able to ascertain, but finds elsewhere in northwestern Europe suggest that opium was in widespread use by this stage, as was cannabis, which is believed to have been infused into fruit and alcoholic concoctions as well as smoked.

The cups from Oakley have incurving rims with openings in the sides that would have enabled them to be suspended from the interior of a roundhouse or swung to increase the smoke. Although such incense cups are more common in Wessex burials, their use seems to have been more widespread, with examples turning up as far afield as East Anglia, Wales, Yorkshire and Scotland.

While dozens, possibly hundreds of burial mounds in this area close to the Dorset Cursus have been ploughed out, this triangle of ground has remained uncultivated pasture for thousands of years. Its long, bleached grass continues to nourish sheep from a nearby farm, as it must have done when the barrows' occupants were living nearby.

Lambourn Seven Barrows Berkshire

Although topography is a constant throughout the ages, the appearance of a landscape may have changed considerably since prehistoric times. This was certainly case with a secluded, dry combe winding north from Lambourn village in Berkshire, which is nowadays dominated by racehorse gallops, but would, five thousand years ago, have been flanked by woodland cradling a chalk stream whose source lay at the head of the valley.

The spot where the water emerged from the ground is marked by the presence nearby of an Early Neolithic long barrow, hinting at settlement dating back to the end of the third millennium BC. Later, in the Early Bronze Age, around forty grave mounds of various sizes (considerably more than the eponymous seven) were built on the valley floor, arranged in two main rows as a kind of processional route that converged on the spring and the long barrow.

A glance at a river map of Britain shows that the stream would have flowed south for a mile or two into the River Lambourn, which at Newbury meets the River Kennet, a major tributary of the Thames.

Thus it would have been possible to row in a dugout canoe from here to the open sea. Such a long, sinuous waterway would have connected communities with each other, the coast and the wider world. Trade would have been conducted along it and perhaps journeys to visit married daughters, to attend weddings and religious ceremonies. Little wonder its birthplace was considered by the region's elite as an auspicious place to be buried.

Bronze Age cemeteries often reveal forgotten geographies like this, over-layered in our minds by modern roads and train lines.

Poor Lot and Bronkham Hill Dorset

Another important Bronze Age barrow cemetery ranged around a long-disappeared stream adorns the sides of a combe to the west of Dorchester in Dorset. As at Lambourn (see previouse spread), the presence of flowing water in prehistory is implied by the lie of the land. But further echoes are to be found in several local villages featuring the name 'Winterbourne', meaning 'seasonal stream'. During the wetter months, the chalklands hereabouts function as aquifers, releasing water as they become saturated. In the distant past when levels were generally higher, these would have been perennial and an important source of water for the area's inhabitants and their livestock.

Viewed from the air, the choice of Poor Lot as sacred ground is immediately explicable. The largest barrows – including examples of the very rare 'pond' type – line up along a raised area overlooking a spot on the valley floor where two streams would have met. These now invisible watercourses have been buried under tarmac, but the aerial perspective yields a vivid sense of their place in the prehistoric landscape.

The bird's-eye view also shows up the presence in neighbouring fields of curious indentations. These are not ploughed-out barrows, as they might appear, but 'dolines' – naturally occurring sinkholes created by the corrosive action of acidic rainwater on the chalk bedrock. There are numerous examples of barrow cemeteries in this region located amid such depressions – notably at nearby Bronkham Hill (right), on the Dorset Ridgeway close to the Hardy Monument, where the burial mounds appear as upturned versions of the hollows beside them.

The occurrence of so many dolines around the meeting point of two streams must have appeared doubly auspicious to people in the Early Bronze Age, a period when water featured prominently in ritual life. Confluences remain important places of worship in many religious traditions today, notably Hinduism, where rivers are personified as female deities and their meeting points regarded as powerful places of healing. It is not inconceivable that similar beliefs prevailed in Britain five thousand years ago.

Priddy Nine Barrows North Hill, Somerset

If you were to formulate a list of qualities that a place should possess in order to be designated as a sacred site in the Bronze Age, North Hill, near the village of Priddy on the Mendip Plateau of Somerset, would tick every box.

At around 300 metres (1,000 feet) in altitude, the hill is among the highest points in the Mendips, thus closer to the sky and heavens than any land around it. A stone's throw away to the north, the presence of four enormous henges in fields pockmarked by sinkholes provides a powerful connection with the underworld and ancestors, while between the two main ridges of North Hill sits an area of low-lying bog. Liminal, porous places, where water seeps into the ground, held great fascination for people throughout prehistory, and this particular marsh must have been especially revered as it drains into the mysterious, vast cave system running beneath nearby Cheddar Gorge, eventually emerging from the mouth of the canyon as a rushing stream that, given its spectacular backdrop of limestone escarpments, must have seemed a great wonder to the area's ancient inhabitants.

These features, along with the proximity of Priddy – whose flat, sheltered situation on the south side of the plateau would have made it appealing as a camp ground to the herders who grazed their flocks up here – may explain why the two parallel ridges of North Hill hold lines of impressive burial mounds.

Amid the group to the south (known as the 'Priddy Nine Barrows') a team of archaeologists from the University of Worcester discovered vestiges of an Early Neolithic causewayed enclosure. The linear cemetery on the opposite, north ridge (the 'Ashen Hill Barrows'), seems, when viewed from the air, to be aligned with a prominent outlier of the Mendip Hills, Crook Peak.

Travelling around this windswept upland, the twin rows of barrows often appear unexpectedly silhouetted on hillcrests – evocative reminders that the old droveways, tracks and heaths up here have been in continual use for six thousand years, and in some cases, considerably longer than that.

Cley Hill Warminster, Wiltshire

Between the limestone uplands of the Mendips and Salisbury Plain to their east rises a lone outlier of chalk known as 'Cley Hill'. Two prominent round barrows dating from the Early Bronze Age adorn its summit. The larger of the pair is visible for miles in every direction, creating a watchful, benevolent presence for the inhabitants of the nearby towns of Frome and Warminster.

How can we interpret summit cairns such as these? At one level, they functioned as simple grave markers, commemorating the lives of valued, high-status individuals or (where multiple burials are involved) lineages. At another, they might have served to reinforce the connection between the people responsible for creating the barrow and the land around it. This early in the Bronze Age, few permanent settlements seem to have existed. Families would have been on the move for most of the year between seasonal camps, though they would doubtless have felt an affinity with the most prominent landforms in their traditional grazing areas.

Something more subtle may also have been in play here. Wonderful viewpoints re-energize the mind and body, promoting a sense of calm and belonging. Because they lived outdoors, our ancestors would have been highly sensitive to the way different places (and the physical effort required to reach them) affected consciousness and mood. Feelings of grief are soothed by spending time on windy hilltops, and this may in part explain why so many in the west of Britain were singled out as funerary sites.

The Rowbarrows Codsend Moor, Exmoor

One of the largest concentrations of Bronze Age funerary cairns in Britain is to be found on Exmoor, straddling the borders of Somerset and Devon. Dunkery Beacon, its culminating point, is crowned with a particularly huge mound, but many smaller ones punctuate the ancient path running along the great whaleback ridge to the west.

The view from this high ground – labelled on OS maps as Codsend Moor – is extraordinary. Beyond the Bristol Channel to the north, the Brecon Beacons undulate across the horizon, petering out in the far west, only to revive for one final flourish at the Preseli Hills, while to the south rises the brooding bulk of Dartmoor.

Hiking along the ridge path, patrolled these days by herds of shaggy Exmoor ponies, you encounter a succession of pale-grey, Early Bronze Age cairns, most of them swathed in bracken and purple heather and difficult to pick out from the ground. With a drone, however, the extent and majesty of this sprawling prehistoric cemetery become apparent.

While the larger, rockier cairns – collectively known as the 'Rowbarrows' – nose above the vegetation, numerous smaller ones show merely as faint circles in the undergrowth. One wonders how many more there may be lurking beneath the carpet of vegetation.

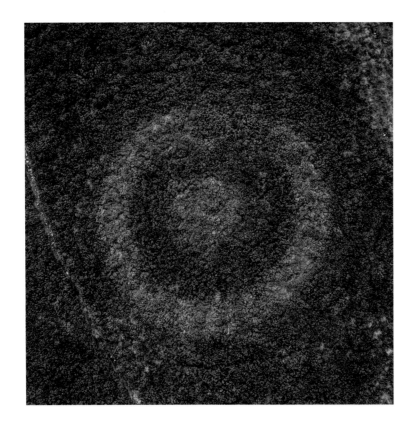

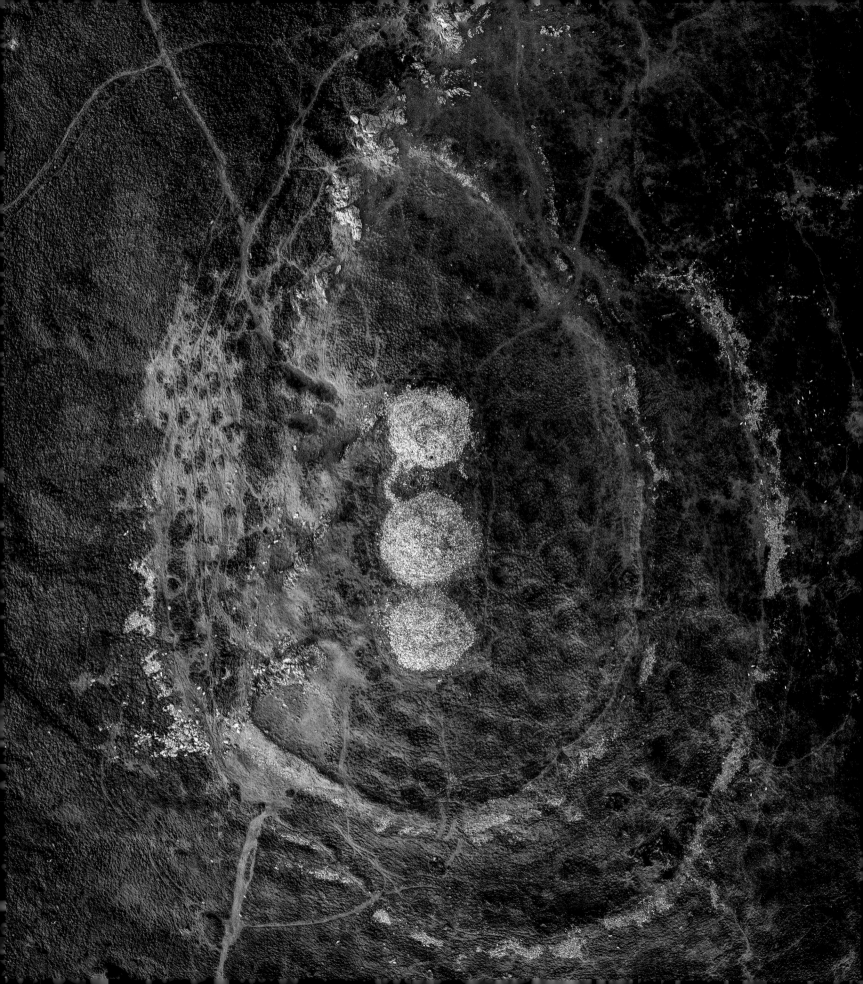

Foel Drygarn Crymych, Pembrokeshire

Among the most striking examples of drystone cairns in Britain is the trio of massive mounds resting on the summit of Foel Drygarn, in the Preseli Hills of Pembrokeshire. This tract of high moorland (or more accurately the rock outcrops that blister at intervals from its flanks) was the source of the spotted dolerite, or 'bluestone', used to create the first incarnation of Stonehenge around 3000 BC, and it clearly remained of great ritual significance to local people in subsequent centuries.

On a clear day, the views from the Preseli summits extend over 160 kilometres (100 miles) west across the sea to the Wicklow Hills in Ireland, north over Cardigan Bay to Snowdonia, and east across the Brecon Beacons and Bristol Channel as far as Exmoor and the Cornish coast.

Foel Drygarn (literally 'the Three Cairns Mountain') forms the high point on the east side of the massif. Sabine Baring-Gould, an Anglican priest from Devon and noted antiquarian, folklorist and novelist, led a dig here in the 1890s, but the team focused their attention on the 227 hut circles crammed on to the hilltop rather than the cairns. These imprints of ancient homes – clearly visible in the 'top down' image opposite – lie within two concentric rings of drystone ramparts erected in the Iron Age, when Foel Drygarn was the first in a chain of four forts ending at St David's Head.

Very little of note came to light in the dig beyond a collection of stone spindle whorls, and a handful of glass beads and jet rings thought to date from the Romano-British era. But this exposed spot at the top of the Preselis, most easily accessible via the nearby village of Crymych, remains a wonderful place to watch the sun set and contemplate how life might have been on the windy edge of Wales two or three thousand years ago.

Nantlle Ridge Snowdonia

Cradled by some of the highest crags in Wales, the grandiose Nantlle Valley offers one of the most direct routes from the Gwynedd coast to the heart of Snowdonia. Mountainsides of green pasture interlaced by ancient stone walls sweep at sheer gradients from the valley floor, scattered with hill farms, ruined copper mines and deserted slate quarries.

A series of large Early Bronze Age cairns overlooks the valley from the great Nantlle Ridge – two of them on the summit of Y Garn. Backed by a dramatic wall of dark peaks, these grave markers barely warrant a mention in most walking guides to the area, perhaps because they are believed to be of relatively recent vintage. But they are probably over four thousand years old and must have taken many years to assemble.

When making the climb to them from the valley floor, it is easy to imagine our forebears making the same ascent – perhaps with a body and pyre wood strapped to a bier, or carrying a large urn of cremated remains – as ravens soared on the thermals rising from the tarns below. On reaching the summit cairns, the reason this inaccessible balcony was favoured soon becomes apparent: the vista north to Mynydd Mawr and Snowdon, buttressed by their angular ridges and immense, blue-grey scree slopes, is simply astounding.

Such monuments provide a powerful connection with our ancestors, reminding us that they appreciated the drama of the Welsh landscape every bit as much as we do today.

Llyn Brenig Denbighshire

Occasionally Bronze Age barrow cemeteries evolved into more complex sites with multiple focal points, creating what archaeologists sometimes refer to as a 'ritual landscape'. Ceremonies at such places probably involved processions via delineated routes, marked by standing stones and, in some cases, timber palisades that served as screens or partitions. This practice would see its fullest expression at Stonehenge, but even prototypical examples became surprisingly elaborate and extensive.

A prime example is a collection of around fifty separate monuments dotted around the shores of Llyn Brenig, a reservoir high on the moorlands dividing Denbighshire and Conwy in North Wales. Created in the 1970s to manage the flow of the River Dee, the lake sits at the top of a valley that would, prior to construction of the dam, have been drained by a fast-flowing mountain stream.

On its eastern side, most of the sites – an assemblage of carefully constructed ring, kerb and platform cairns holding several cremation burials each – are made of stone. On the west flank of the valley, however, the heather and bracken are strewn with more classic earth-and-turf round barrows. Between them, archaeologists discovered the vestiges of several wooden palisades, suggesting some kind of division may have existed between a 'land of the living' (symbolized by wood) and the 'land of the ancestors' (made largely of stone).

It seems likely the whole formed a kind of ceremonial circuit for mourners performing cremation rituals. Its modern equivalent, an 'archaeological trail' inaugurated by the county council, nowadays provides easy access to the main monuments, a few of which have been restored to give an impression of their original scale and appearance.

Dated 2000–1500 BC, the monument pictured here (known as 'Brenig 44') is a stone ring cairn that was originally surrounded by timber posts (the sites of which are now marked by stakes). Three cremation burials were discovered within it.

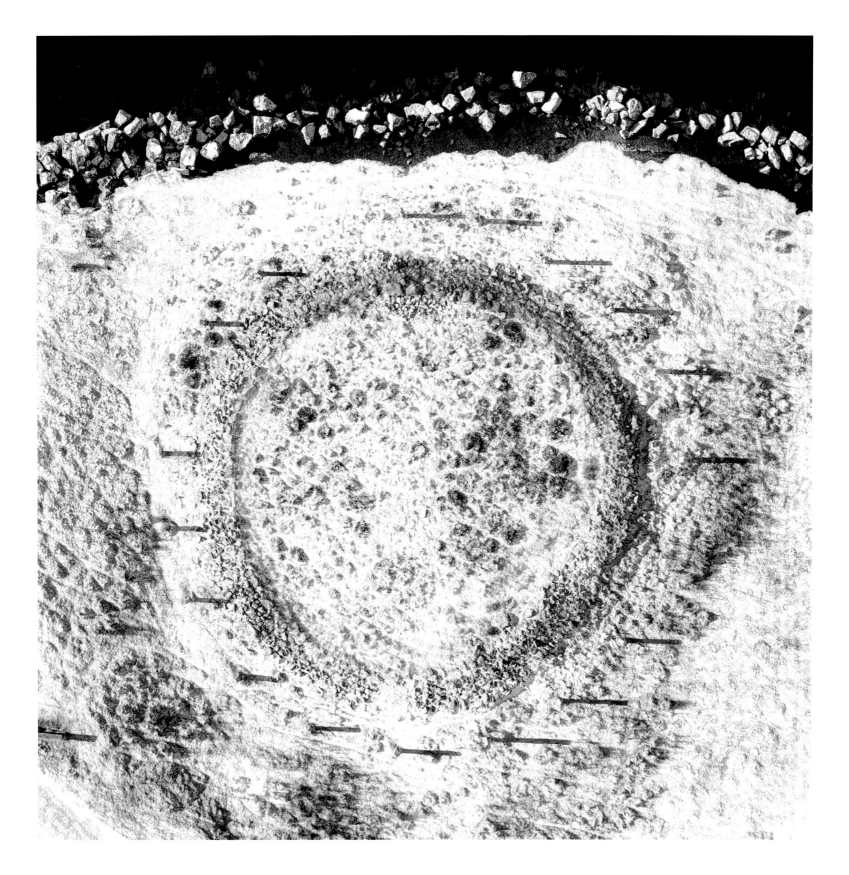

Moel Goedog Ardudwy, Gwynedd

Another fine example of a Bronze Age processional route
extends from the coast of North Wales near Harlech across
a somewhat forgotten but very beautiful upland area in the
lap of the Rhinog Mountains called Ardudwy.

Punctuated by a sequence of standing stones and ring
cairns, the track today scythes over pasture enclosed by
an expansive quilt of drystone walls before scaling the
flanks of a prominent hill crowned by a fort. Surrounded
by two concentric earth ditches and banks, the site has
never received much attention from archaeologists, but its
resemblance to others in the region reliably dated to the
Early Bronze Age suggest it is of considerable antiquity.

Several large cremation urns were discovered in the
ring cairns on the slopes below, hinting at this windswept
hillside's importance as a funerary site. Gazing across
Tremadoc Bay and the Glaslyn Estuary to the hills of the
Llŷn Peninsula and, due north, to Snowdon, it is easy to see
why. Few viewpoints in Wales encompass such a spectrum
of different terrains, and Moel Goedog feels like a pivotal
landform in the middle of them – a quality our Bronze Age
ancestors frequently sought out.

Bryn Cader Faner Ardudwy, Gwynedd

It may be just one tenth of the size of Stonehenge, but this ring cairn high in the Rhinog mountains of North Wales casts a powerful spell.

Dating from the end of the third millennium BC, the monument is the culmination of an ancient trackway winding from the coast between Harlech and Barmouth via a tangle of drystone walls, gurgling streams and pockets of disused manganese mine workings. After a steady climb, the path, now helpfully waymarked, crests a ridge to enter a hidden combe speckled with tarns of inky, dark water, overlooked from the north by a grassy knoll on which our ancestors assembled their masterpiece.

Despite being robbed by medieval treasure hunters and later used as target practice by soldiers training in World War II, Bryn Cader Faner remains a precious relic from the Early Bronze Age, one whose power derives as much from its extraordinary location as its unique, crown-like appearance. The eighteen slabs encircling the cairn were deliberately set at an angle, inclined outwards (there would originally have been at least thirty). Resembling slender fingers stretching up to the heavens, the tilted stones create a pivotal point around which the landscape appears to revolve. The sight line with distant Snowdon, due north of Bryn Cader Faner, feels particularly significant.

Moel Ty Uchaf Denbighshire

The remnants of another superbly situated ring cairn adorn a natural balcony high above the Dee Valley in Denbighshire, on the north side of the Berwyn mountains – a tract of high, rather forbidding moorland that forms an outer rampart for the higher peaks of Snowdonia beyond.

Like Bryn Cader Faner (see previous spread), its location must have been chosen for the expansive views that stretch from the site, encompassing ranks of shadowy ridges and deep valleys latticed by drystone walls where, in early spring, the bleating of ewes and their lambs fills their air (as it has done for over five thousand years in this region).

Around forty stones, with an opening aligned to the midwinter solstice sunset, are today all that's left of a monument that must in its day have been an impressive spectacle. It is tempting to picture gatherings of local Bronze Age herders up here in their sheepskin cloaks, making offerings, intoning prayers and stoking sacred fires as the shadows lengthened and the last rays of midwinter sunlight spilled over the cairn – though in reality we have no clues as to the nature of ceremonies performed here, nor what beliefs framed them.

Superstitions have continued to swirl around the structure in modern times. In January 1974, Moel Ty Uchaf made national headlines after local people reported sightings of bright lights, explosions and special forces at work in the area. Rumours circulated that a spaceship had crash landed and that the bodies of its alien crew had been spirited away by the government – a mystery referred to in the British media at the time as 'the Welsh Roswell' (after the mysterious downing in 1847 of a military balloon on an army base in Roswell, New Mexico, which was associated by many with UFO sightings in the area).

Regardless of how much truth there may have been in these reports, the fact that such unexplained events were perceived to have been connected with the remote circle of stones demonstrates the power such sites continue to exert on the popular imagination.

The Over Narrows Cambridgeshire Fens

Most archaeological digs in Britain these days are prompted (and financed) by development projects. It is an uncomfortable irony, but at least the sites and their significance end up being better understood before they are destroyed by road building, quarrying or construction. In fact, many wouldn't have been discovered at all were it not for the support from the developers involved. This was the case with some amazing finds outside the village of Over in the Cambridgeshire Fens, where gravel extraction work in the 1990s and early 2000s led to the uncovering of a ceremonial landscape on a grand scale.

Three to four thousand years ago, the Great Ouse River flowed across the East Anglian floodplain in a series of sweeping oxbow meanders. Long, narrow ridges rising to around 3 metres (10 feet) above the water ran across this delta, and these were clearly attractive to prehistoric people across the ages, yielding a wealth of archaeological finds, from Mesolithic flint scatters to Neolithic henges, Bronze Age settlement middens and ritual depositions connected to an Iron Age shrine. The latter involved the remains of numerous human body parts, dismembered horses and what appeared to be rare examples of bird sacrifice.

However, the largest features investigated by the Cambridge Archaeological Unit, who ran the dig at Over, were a collection of barrows dating from the Early Bronze Age. Holding more than forty cremations, the mounds (two of which were waterlogged) formed part of a complex featuring huge screens made from telegraph-pole-sized posts. An estimated 4 hectares (10 acres) of forest must have been cleared to create them – a massive engineering project requiring the participation of many individuals. The purpose of the timbers appears to have been to frame sight lines of the barrows from the opposite shore of the river, suggesting – as with the sites covered on preceding pages – that movement through the monuments formed an integral part of the activities carried out within and around them.

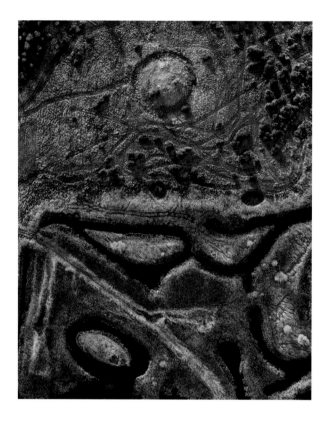

This was the kind of terrain often categorized by archaeologists as 'liminal' – an edgeland where water and earth intermingle. Quite why these landscapes exerted such fascination for our Bronze Age ancestors is a matter of speculation, but it does seem as if wetlands and marshes were regarded as a kind of proxy for the border between the realm of the living and the afterlife – a portal to the mysteries and powers of the underworld, perhaps?

Since the Great Ouse was drained and channelled in the 1600s, this particular liminal landscape has altered dramatically. Modern gravel extraction has created an elaborate palimpsest of landforms and vegetation that offer a striking spectacle from the air.

Hingston Cairn and Stone Row Dartmoor, Devon

Dartmoor retains one of the most remarkable collections of Bronze Age sites anywhere in Europe, dating from an era when the uplands supported a thriving population of herders who grazed their livestock on what was then abundant grassland. After a combination of climate change and environmental overload brought this way of life to an end around 1000 BC, the settlers moved to lower, sheltered valleys, leaving the moorland to degenerate into acidic peat bog.

The empty expanses of bracken, sedge and cotton grass, broken by low hills crowned with outcrops of eroded granite tors, today form an evocative backdrop for the numerous ceremonial sites surviving from the late third and early second millennium BC.

In addition to some striking stone circles and cairns, the moors are marked with long avenues of menhirs, believed to have served as processional walkways aligned with auspicious landforms or points on the near horizon where the sun or moon rose at key moments in the annual calendar. Often, these monuments derive much of their drama from the surrounding landscape, whose topography they serve to accentuate.

A prime example is a 349-metre (1,149-foot) long stone row hidden in a high natural amphitheatre above Burrator Reservoir, on the southwest side of Dartmoor. Beginning with orthostats of around knee height, the megaliths of the Hingston Stone Row grow in stature as they march down the bracken-covered slope, cross a dry stream bed and climb the opposite hillside towards their culminating point: a beautiful ring cairn enclosed by a kerb of twenty-five upright stones, seeming to form an elegant sweep

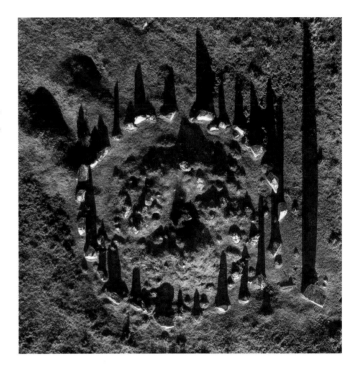

that mirrors the curves of the moor. The overall effect is mesmerizing.

It is tempting to picture large numbers of people processing around the avenue, dressed in their Bronze Age finery as onlookers watched from the outcrops above. Was this a site to which people travelled from afar, or one used only by the local herders whose hut circles and enclosures litter the hillside below nearby Down Tor?

Boscawen Un St Buryan, Cornwall

If barrow complexes are the defining feature of the south and east of Britain in the Early Bronze Age, then stone circles were their equivalent in the north and west. And you can't get much further west in Britain that Boscawen Un, a gem of a ceremonial structure not far from Land's End, in an area known as West Penwith. This distant corner of Cornwall is rich in ancient sites, spanning almost four thousand years of prehistory. Boscawen Un dates from the Chalcolithic, or Copper Age, when knowledge of metal making first entered Britain, but when the way of life still remained largely rooted in the traditions of the Neolithic.

The site comprises eighteen grey granite upright stones and one of gleaming white quartz, arrayed around a central menhir deliberately set at an angle. The latter sports a faint and rare petroglyph on its lower flank, depicting an axe head (similar in form to those carved on to one of the Stonehenge trilithons, and which have, from their style, led some scholars to posit a connection with Mycenae in Homeric-era Greece).

Potent as a symbol of male and female fertility, the ensemble is today wreathed in high hedgerows that obscure the sunrise. In its day, however, during the week around the autumn equinox the shadow cast by the central stone would have touched the white stone to the west.

Astronomical alignments such as this are a common feature of stone circles, though it is not always easy to establish what the cosmological connection was. The white quartz stone at Boscawen may equally indicate the position of the rising or setting moon at a key point in the annual lunar cycle.

No doubt the numinous quality of the white rock, and the fact that it emits a magical green spark when struck, would have fascinated our Bronze Age ancestors, who frequently deposited flakes of knapped or crushed quartz in graves. Across the world and through different ages, quartz is also closely connected to the practices of shamans and shamanism.

Last, but perhaps most significant of all in this context, quartz is an essential ingredient for making moulds and crucibles used in metal casting. Because it melts at a much higher temperature than copper or tin, the mineral tempered the clay moulds used by our ancestors to make axes, knives and swords. Quite simply, without it there would have been no Bronze Age.

Ballowall Barrow (Carn Gluze) Cape Cornwall

Dramatically set close to a granite cliff edge on the Land's End Peninsula, the Ballowall Barrow (also known by its Cornish name, Carn Gluze) lay under a heap of spoil from the nearby mines until a local antiquarian and MP named William Copeland Borlase cleared away the debris in 1878. The enormous barrow he found, 22 metres (72 feet) in diameter, comprised two concentric walls, inside which were set five stone-lined cists containing pottery and cremated human remains.

Restoration work subsequently carried out by Borlase radically altered the appearance of the barrow, which would originally have been surmounted by an impressive dome of dry stones. Unusually for a structure of its kind, it was later found to have been erected over the top of a much older Neolithic tomb.

By the time the cairn saw its final phase of use in the Middle Bronze Age, this remote edge of Cornwall was among Europe's principal sources of tin. The metal was probably first recognized in the late third millennium BC by cross-Channel traders or prospectors from Armorica (Brittany) or,

more likely, the Tagus River region of southwest Iberia. The ore occurs in exposed seams in cliffs and river banks and has a dark purple hue that would have made it relatively easy to identify.

Tin is extremely rare in Europe and was in great demand by the voracious city-states of the Eastern Mediterranean. Archaeological evidence suggests that by around 2000 BC the metal was being smelted and moulded into bun-shaped ingots at settlements across Cornwall and Dartmoor for export from a port named in later Greek and Latin sources as 'Ictis' – thought to be Mount Batten in Plymouth Harbour (or, possibly, nearby St Michael's Mount).

The scale of the trade is hard to estimate, but bronze containing Cornish tin has been found in wrecks off the coast of Israel (contemporary with the late Minoan period of Crete). Isotopic analysis has also shown that both tin and gold gathered in West Penwith was used to make the famous Nebra Sky Disc discovered in Germany – the earliest known depiction of the cosmos, dated to the sixteenth century BC.

Great Orme Llandudno, Conwy

That prospectors or traders searching for copper crossed the Irish Sea from the Continent (probably southwest Iberia) midway through the third millennium BC we know from the remains of Early Bronze Age mines on Ross Island, in County Kerry. Open-cast mining work began on this peninsula on Loch Learne around 2400 BC, and by 2200 BC copper was also being extracted across the water in Wales (principally from Parys Mountain in Anglesey and Cwmystwyth near Aberystwyth).

By far the richest source of British copper in the Bronze Age, however, was the mighty limestone peninsula overlooking what is now Llandudno, on Wales's north coast. Here, mining began on a small scale around 1700 BC, but within a century, vast quantities of ore were being dug

from a labyrinthine network of galleries and tunnels extending 70 metres (230 feet) underground.

A staggering 175 to 238 tonnes of copper is estimated to have been produced at Great Orme before the workings fell into disuse at the start of the Iron Age (around 900 BC). Mining on this scale could not have been an ad hoc, seasonal undertaking – as is likely to have been the case elsewhere –

but would have required a full-time, specialist workforce who lived nearby and processed the ore in situ.

Tools discovered in the Bronze Age tunnels indicate most of the mining was done with large hammer stones sourced on local beaches. Fire would have been used to fracture the ore-rich rock, and wedges made from animal bone or hardwood inserted into the cracks formed after water had been used to cool it. A sophisticated ventilation system must also have been installed to remove the resulting smoke, while groundwater would have been expelled via a network of wooden gutters (examples of which have survived in other prehistoric mines in Wales).

Even so, conditions underground must have been horrific and loss of life frequent.

Kilmartin Glen Argyll

Striking evidence of the impact made on mainland Britain by the boom in Irish copper production over the final centuries of the third millennium BC survives in a secluded valley on Scotland's wild northwest coast, near the village of Kilmartin.

Open to the sea on one side and sheltered by rugged highland crags on the other three, the glen in question has a broad, level floor whose mineral-rich, easily cultivable soil must have made it something of a breadbasket three to four thousand years ago. From this prosperous base, the valley's inhabitants were able to dominate trade between Ireland and the populous northeast of Scotland via the Great Glen.

We know that Kilmartin served as an important entrepôt for Ross Island copper during the Chalcolithic period from the prevalence of finely made and decorated, Irish-style terracotta food vessels discovered in Early Bronze Age contexts here, along with several beautiful red copper daggers (made from Killarney copper). Over time, the chiefly lineage who ruled the glen appear to have grown exceptionally powerful and wealthy on the back of this trade, lavishing resources on a crop of elaborate funerary cairns and luxury items to place in them (notably spacer-plate necklaces made from highly polished black Whitby jet).

Towards the end of the Bronze Age, after the region's climate became colder and wetter, the old Bronze Age floor of Kilmartin Glen acquired a layer of peat that submerged its prehistoric monuments until the bog was drained and cleared in the nineteenth century. Once the old cairns were exposed, much of their stonework was removed by local landowners for masonry, but much survives.

Today, the linear cemetery of cairns forms the centrepiece of a remarkable storehouse of prehistoric sites, ranging from Neolithic standing stones and rock art sites to Scotland's oldest stone circles. A small museum in Kilmartin village provides an overview of the area's monuments. The glen's greatest treasures – the famous jet necklaces and bronze bracelets unearthed in the great cairns – reside in the National Museum of Scotland, Edinburgh.

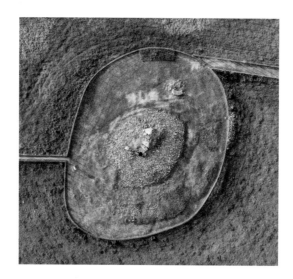

Loanhead of Daviot Inverurie, Aberdeenshire

At the opposite, northeast end of the Great Glen from Kilmartin, the rolling country between the Cairngorm mountains and the coast of Aberdeenshire was an area well populated in the Early and Middle Bronze Age. The defining prehistoric monument of this area is the 'recumbent stone circle', a style of funerary structure unique to the region comprising a ring of orthostats with a large, rectangular monolith at its apex flanked by a pair of uprights. Inside this is usually found a drystone platform or ring cairn built over a cist holding cremated remains.

A particularly well-preserved example survives on a hilltop outside the village of Daviot, to the north of Inverurie. The monument's outer circle consists of nine upright stones and an impressive recumbent, bookended by the usual pair of flankers – one stout and one taller and more slender – a juxtaposition suggestive of 'male' and 'female'. The cairn inside is ringed by a low kerb. When it was excavated in the 1930s, the site was found to contain the remains of a funeral pyre dating from the Early Bronze Age, though other deposits were inserted at later dates.

Around seventy such recumbent circles are to be found in this region. The majority of them have direct lines of sight to a hill known today as 'Bennachie', whose significance may derive from the distinctive breast-like shape of its principal summit, Mither Tap (Scots for 'Mother Top'; Bennachie is Gaelic for 'Hill of the Breast'). Thanks to a plantation of trees now screening the circle, the connection between Loanhead of Daviot and the sacred Bronze Age mountain in the distance is not immediately apparent at ground level, but may clearly be discerned from above.

Clava Cairns of Balnuaran and Corrimony Inverness-shire

Corrimony

Another type of cairn crops up extensively in the country to the north and west of Aberdeenshire, around the shores of the Moray Firth. It is often described as the 'Clava' style, after a famous site on the banks of the River Nairn, to the east of Inverness.

Balnuaran of Clava, to give it its full name, is a linear cemetery dating from the Early Bronze Age (around 2200 BC). Only three cairns survive today, but many more would probably have lined the floor of this verdant, shallow vale before they fell prey to the plough. Those at Balnuaran are today protected by a beech coppice planted more than a century ago by a local laird – a keen antiquarian and lover of Romantic poetry who wished to create a 'Druidic bower' with which to amuse his visitors.

Two distinct styles are represented here: cairns with narrow passage entrances that would once have been surmounted by corbelled drystone roofs; and a large ring cairn with no entrance, whose central chamber may have been open to the sky, or perhaps enclosed by a capstone. Both are surrounded by substantial kerbs incorporating cup-marked rocks (carved during the earlier Neolithic period) and circles of large upright stones. The latter grow larger and redder on their southwest sides, facing the midwinter solstice sunset, and smaller and paler on the opposite, northeast side.

An hour's drive southwest of Balnuaran, up a narrow valley running towards Glen Affric from Loch Ness, is another beautiful Clava-style monument, known as the 'Corrimony Cairn'. It was excavated in the 1950s by Stuart Pigott and his team, who lifted off the cup-marked capstone to reveal a burial chamber lined with water-worn cobbles from the adjacent stream. Beneath it, a layer of compacted sand was stained by the outlines of a crouched burial, thought to have been that of a woman. Hundreds of fragments of white quartz had been scattered over and around her body, along with pieces of charcoal and the remains of what appeared to be a funerary feast.

Burderop Celtic Fields Wiltshire

Midway through the second millennium BC, roughly seven or eight centuries after the bronze revolution began in Britain, significant changes started taking place in these islands – changes that would leave a lasting impression on the country's landscape.

Ceremonial structures such as stone circles, cairns and barrows gradually disappear from the archaeological record. Clearly, the elite whose remains and treasures were buried in the linear cemeteries of Wessex, for example, no longer felt the need to articulate their power and prestige through monument building. At the same time, a mass of luxurious weaponry and armour begins to turn up in rivers, lakes and marshes around the country, where they appear to have been placed as some form of ritual sacrifice.

The scale and number of these hoards show that vast quantities of metal were being crafted into luxury items at around this time. Often made of 'softer' alloys (with a high lead content) showing no signs of wear and tear, these were made more for display than practical use. Moreover, the people to whom all these beautiful swords, spears and shields belonged must have accumulated considerable surplus in order to acquire them. But how did they obtain it?

The answer is hinted at in the appearance, at around the same time as ritual deposition gathered pace in Britain, of distinct field systems – regularly spaced, man-made boundaries dug to drain land and denote its limits of ownership. Communities were directing considerable effort into such endeavours, suggesting that whoever was controlling them enjoyed significant coercive power.

One of the best preserved of these Middle to Late Bronze Age field systems cascades down a chalk slope just outside Swindon in Wiltshire. Although in use well into the Iron Age, the so-called 'Celtic Fields of Burderop' reveal how the hillside was reshaped by constant ploughing from the late second millennium onwards.

Seeing this chequerboard from above, you gain a vivid sense of how agriculture was intensifying through the Late Bronze Age. As farming grew more productive and efficient, food supply would have become more secure. Populations grew steadily, providing ever greater numbers of people to till the soil, care for livestock and pay tithes to the overlords (the source of the wealth used to acquire ostentatious bronze items and host feasts). This was, in effect, the engine room of a boom that would, over the ensuing centuries, totally transform both the appearance of the British countryside and the way of life it supported.

Leskernick Hill Bodmin Moor, Cornwall

The rise in population and emergence of land enclosure across much of Britain from 1500 BC coincided with a general warming of the climate, which enabled people to inhabit uplands such as Dartmoor and Bodmin.

As evidenced by sites such as Hingston Cairn (see p. 165), villages appeared at sheltered spots on the moorlands, giving rise to what must have been a unique way of life. Some particularly evocative vestiges of the era survive at Leskernick, a large, oval-shaped hill at the heart of Bodmin Moor scattered with myriad granite boulders and stones. Among the so-called 'clitter' of rocks on its west and southern flanks nestle two Bronze Age settlements consisting of around forty hut circles, and their associated drystone livestock enclosures and field boundaries.

Encircled on all sides by higher ground, Leskernick feels today like a place apart. You have to walk a long way to get there, and when you arrive, it is immediately apparent why our ancestors favoured the spot. Superb views extend across the moors to the serrated spine of Brown Willy and other tor-topped hills dominating the horizon.

We know from the placement of stone rows and circles in the valley below that these landforms were venerated by the moor's inhabitants in the Neolithic period – a reverence that appears to have been shared by people at Leskernick, many of whose hut circles are orientated towards prominent granite outcrops on the surrounding ridges. Unusual boulders are incorporated into the outlines of some farmsteads, while prominent upright stones are marked by cairns.

The pièce de résistance at Leskernick, however, is a huge propped stone. The installation rests on a giant plinth of naturally occurring granite, tilting at a very deliberate angle with its central axis pointing straight at Rough Tor (see p. 69). The great rock outcrop to the northwest provided the principal focus of worship for people in this area from Early Neolithic times until the end of the Bronze Age, when a dramatic deterioration in climate forced people to more tolerable altitudes.

Dartmoor's Pounds and Reaves Devon

Over 270 Bronze Age settlements have been identified on Dartmoor in South Devon. The uplands may have a forlorn feel today, but three and a half thousand years ago they were teeming with life. Smoke from hundreds of cooking fires and metal-smelting workshops would have plumed over the grasslands, dotted with countless sheep and cattle whose hides and dairy produce would have been transported down the river valleys, along with knuckle-shaped ingots of tin bound via the Tamar for ports on the coast, from where they were exported to the Continent.

A particularly well-preserved example of a Bronze Age village is Grimspound, in the heart of Dartmoor, where twenty-four hut circles are enclosed inside a drystone wall 150 metres (492 feet) wide. Similar 'pounds', as these structures are known locally, crop up at numerous sites in the area, including Drizzlecombe, on the southwest flank of the moor, where they sit alongside a spectacular array of ceremonial cairns, stone rows and giant menhirs dating from the Late Neolithic/Chalcolithic period.

Dartmoor has also become well known among archaeologists for its distinctive coaxial field systems, or 'reaves'. Among the earliest examples of large-scale land enclosure in Britain, these chequerboards of Bronze Age boundary walls frequently bisect or radiate from settlements, or else mark the boundaries between lower, cultivable land and grazing zones on the high moor. Others delineate important watersheds that may have formed boundaries between different communities.

The archaeologist Andrew Fleming, who conducted the first detailed study of reaves in the 1970s and 1980s, has suggested such systems were created over a relatively short time frame to a single 'master plan' that provided a

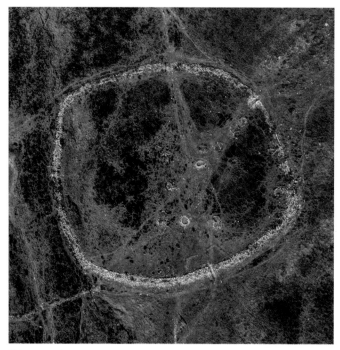

Grimspound

kind of blueprint for comparable enclosures elsewhere in Britain (though in recent years, others have favoured a more piecemeal and episodic construction process).

Fleming's 'blueprint' theory rests heavily on a small number of rather shaky radiocarbon dates, but even if coaxial field enclosure did not originate on Dartmoor, it had an enduring impact on the way land was both managed and perceived in Britain from around 1500 BC to the present day.

Venford Reave, Dartmeet

Drizzlecombe Pounds

The Uffington White Horse Oxfordshire

Galloping across the chalk downs of Oxfordshire, the Uffington White Horse is the oldest surviving hill figure in Britain and, quite simply, one of the great masterpieces of prehistoric art in Europe. Its sweeping lines, spread over 110 metres (360 feet) from head to tail, convey with Picasso-like minimalism the feel of a steed in motion, frozen in mid-stride with its body fully outstretched. How this effect was achieved without the benefit of an aerial perspective remains a mystery, but the work, whose form is hard to fully appreciate at ground level, was clearly intended to be viewed from a distance.

For years, archaeologists believed the horse dated from the Late Iron Age, but soil extracted from the metre-deep trenches dug to create it placed the work at around 1000–800 BC, the very end of the Bronze Age. This was precisely the time when domesticated horses, originally bred on the Pontic-Caspian steppe and brought west by migrants from the Hungarian Plain, first make an appearance in the British archaeological record.

The impact must have been profound. A warhorse decked in polished bronze gear would have been an impressive sight for Britons, and the first animals would have brought enormous prestige to their owners. No wonder, then, that an equestrian image, modelled from vivid white compacted chalk, was chosen as a kind of totemic emblem by the inhabitants of nearby Uffington Castle, one of the region's largest settlements and the most likely place for the makers of the White Horse to have lived.

The figure's precise purpose remains a mystery but the scarp ridge on which it was etched had, from the Early Neolithic period, been used for funerary rituals. Some scholars assert that it may have been intended as a representation of the great solar horse of Celtic mythology, associated with the sun god featured on coins across northwest Europe in the Iron Age.

It is noteworthy that the chalk downs south of the scarp ridge, particularly around the village of Lambourn (see p. 136) are today dominated by racehorse gallops. Did the Uffington White Horse serve as a siren call for all these top trainers and breeders, or is their presence a coincidence?

Iron Age Britain

The arrival of domesticated horses around the turn of the first and second millennium BC, discerned more by the presence of bronze stirrups and other metal gear than actual physical remains (which were scant), coincides with the beginning of the Iron Age in Britain. But iron, while present in a few archaeological contexts from 800 BC onwards, would not be widely adopted for another two or three centuries. Instead, bronze continued to be the metal of choice for ritual depositions, which still occurred on a large scale until the seventh century BC. Quite why this was the case remains uncertain, but we do know the British climate at this time was extremely cold and wet, which may have caused crop failure and other catastrophes requiring propitiation of, and intervention from, the gods.

In the course of the seventh century BC, however, hoarding diminished significantly. More and more land was being taken into production and farmsteads proliferated. As the climate improved and population increased, so distinct regional identities began to emerge across Britain.

The Early Iron Age (800–400 BC)

Quite why – despite being readily available all over the country – it took so long for iron to be fully adopted is a moot point. The explanation probably lay in the intensive nature of forging: tin and copper become molten at relatively low temperatures and can thus be purified and cast through smelting, but to expel its impurities, iron ore has to be repeatedly heated and hammered; and when it cools, the metal looks dark and rather less magical than does bronze.

Once the advantages of the new metal became apparent, however, its uses multiplied and had a transformational impact – not so much on the production of prestige items for the elite, which continued to be made mainly in bronze, but on everyday life.

Tougher and more easily repairable, iron could be used to create tyres for wooden wheels, making wagons and chariots more robust. It made longer, thicker nails, enabling boatbuilders to create sturdier vessels less prone to floundering in the swells of the Atlantic. Iron ploughshares allowed farmers to work heavier soils, cultivate more land, grow more grain and feed more people. Toolboxes of adzes, hammers, chisels and other cutting blades also became commonplace, allowing people to build larger and stronger roundhouses to accommodate the growing population, with far less of an outlay in time and effort.

The Middle Iron Age (400–150 BC)

By the period referred to by archaeologists as the Middle Iron Age, which began in roughly 400 BC, Britain could be divided into three distinct zones, distinguished by their different types of settlement and material culture.

The east, from the Thames to Northumberland, was characterized by open villages and farmsteads. In the west, in a band stretching from Cornwall to the Inner Hebrides, settlements tended to be smaller and more heavily fortified; while between the two, the central zone, from the south coast to North Wales, was dominated by large hillforts.

Surrounded by earth ramparts and ditches, most hillforts were constructed in the sixth and fifth centuries BC. They were primarily defensive structures to begin with, designed to provide a refuge in times of threat, as well as a place to store grain safely, though equally the strongholds would have served as expressions of power and status . Some were also used for religious ceremonies, processions and feasts, with the larger strongholds providing central points around which smaller forts coalesced. Over time, in response to greater instability, the lesser strongholds tended to fall into disuse while the larger ones became more populous and better defended.

Different regions gradually developed their own distinct identities, giving rise to the tribal confederacies that would characterize the Late Iron Age. These cultural differences are most clearly manifest in

Decorative detail from a feasting bucket.

the archaeological record through pottery, but there must have been innumerable other ways in which groups identified themselves, whether through textiles and costume, body paint or hair styles.

By the third century BC, tension in Britain was mounting. Larger walls with deeper ditches, heftier palisades and elaborate gateway fortifications were being added to the hillforts. Archaeological digs have uncovered much evidence of burning and violence from this period: stashes of sling stones, cut marks on skeletons and an increasing number of war chariots and weapons crop up in third-century contexts.

In spite of the growing instability, however, trade gathered pace through the Middle Iron Age and the influence of continental Europe steadily increased. This was the period when what is widely called 'Celtic Art' reaches one of its high points, in what is known as the 'La Tène-style' designs, which originated in northern France but were soon adopted in Britain. Decorated with swirling tendrils, stylized animals and mythical creatures, a wealth of new artefacts, from exquisite parade armour to intricate brooches, were being imported – and then expertly copied by artisans in southern Britain.

The Thames Valley became the principal production centre for these new luxury items, developing in time into a uniquely British style that drew heavily on the La Tène traditions but evolved its own distinct look.

Bound together by these growing trade connections, territories on opposite sides of the Channel started to closely resemble each other. It is likely that regular gift exchange and the movement of brides in both directions underscored this cultural convergence, whether between Kent and northern Gaul or the southwest regions and Armorica (Brittany).

At the same time, the influence of the distant Mediterranean region began to make itself felt. Maritime and river routes around France that had been in regular use since the Neolithic, but which had grown much busier with the tin and copper trades of the Bronze Age, were now being used to acquire metals for the burgeoning markets of the Eastern Mediterranean. The British elite were also developing a taste for the luxuries travelling in the opposite direction: perfume, exotic textiles and foodstuffs such as dried figs and, of course, wine all started to pour into the country in greater quantities.

The Late Iron Age (150 BC–AD 43)

Hengistbury Head, in Christchurch Harbour, emerged as the most important trade hub on the south coast over the course of the second century BC. Originating in the ports of Armorica (Brittany), bronze drinking cups, wine amphorae and glass beads from northern and central Italy have been found in Late Iron Age layers around the old harbour, pointing to the increased influence of Rome on Britain.

Further evidence of this is the appearance on these islands of the first gold coins, minted by the tribes of Belgic Gaul inhabiting the region between the Seine and the Rhine. A significant number found their way into Britain after Julius Caesar invaded Gaul (France) in the Gallic Wars of 58–55 BC, when gold staters were gifted to British warriors in exchange for military support.

Sensing an opportunity, Caesar rounded off his triumphant campaign with two short but seminal forays across the Channel in 55 and 54 BC. Neither yielded much in the way of plunder or territory, but the expeditions did prove it was possible to cross the sea and wage war in the wild lands beyond. The Romans also gained valuable intelligence about the politics of Iron Age Britain, forging allegiances with tribes in the southeast that would prove invaluable a couple of generations later.

The Gallic Wars had a major impact on life in Britain. With Gaul now a fully integrated part of the Roman Empire, trade intensified, though the emphasis shifted: Hengistbury Head went into decline after its main trading partner across the water, Armorica, was destroyed. Instead, the bulk of cross-Channel commerce was funnelled through the southeast, whose tribal capitals became increasingly Romanized. Hillforts in the region were gradually deserted in favour of less heavily defended sites on the banks of major rivers, known as 'oppida'. Within a couple of decades, life in these new market hubs more closely resembled that of Roman Gaul than the hillforts further west in Britain, which held on more tenaciously to the old ways.

Another likely consequence of this quiet revolution was an increase in slavery. Even before the Gallic Wars, hillforts in the central zone, occupied by tribes such as the Durotriges, Belgae and Dubonni, began to acquire new and more formidable defences. The most likely explanation is that smaller strongholds were being raided and their inhabitants taken as slaves destined for the markets of Rome. Those who survived the raids would have fled to the larger hillforts, such as Maiden Castle and Hod Hill in Dorset.

The southeastern tribes, meanwhile, continued to embrace Roman culture with increasing enthusiasm, growing more prosperous on the back of booming trade with Gaul. To the Emperor Claudius, casting a covetous eye beyond the northern borders of his empire, Britain – or at least the bottom right-hand corner of it – must have seemed like low-hanging fruit.

Carn Euny, Cornwall

Conquest

The Claudian conquest of AD 43 got off to an inauspicious start. Spooked by the prospect of crossing the Channel, the 40,000 legionnaires and camp followers who had gathered at the port of Gesoriacum (modern-day Boulogne) staged a mutiny. By the end of the summer, however, the Roman army had successfully taken the main oppidum of Camulodunum (Colchester) and formed a bridgehead from which the legions pushed west over the succeeding years.

The tribes of the periphery – including the Durotriges, who resisted the Roman advance through Dorset – were subjugated by the end of the decade, followed by Wales in the AD 70s and Scotland in AD 84.

In an incredibly short time, the rich, multifaceted 'Celtic' culture that had evolved in a largely unbroken fashion over thousands of years was brought to an abrupt end. The hillforts were emptied or remodelled for use as Roman forts. Roads were built to facilitate the movement

Barbury, Wiltshire

Winklebury, Wiltshire

of troops and supplies between strategically placed garrison towns. And the old shrines and deities were replaced by their Roman counterparts – in some cases, such as Maiden Castle near Dorchester and Casterley Camp near Stonehenge, by building temples actually inside former hillforts.

The written histories of Tacitus and Julius Caesar record that some Britons escaped and fled west and north into unconquered territories to ally with other tribes and continue the resistance. But of the songs, stories, sagas and mythologies that entertained them in their roundhouses before the arrival of the legions, only a few echoes survive (mostly in epic poems from early medieval Welsh and Irish literature).

Ritual and Beliefs in the Iron Age

There's a reason why this section of the book is given over almost entirely to photographs of hillforts and roundhouses. Whereas the remnants of previous eras of prehistory were mostly religious or ceremonial in nature, the only Iron Age sites visible from the air today were essentially defensive, agricultural or domestic. The beliefs framing people's lives are, however, discernible to an extent in the archaeological record, and alluded to in the chronicles of Classical writers such as Julius Caesar, Strabo and Tacitus, among others.

Caesar's account of the Gallic wars, *Bellum Gallicum*, includes several passages devoted to the Druids, a priestly class who enforced

traditional law and acted as intermediaries between the gods and men in Iron Age Gaul and Britain. Tacitus describes their activities in particularly lurid terms, with numerous references to human sacrifice. 'It was their religion,' he wrote, 'to drench their altars in the blood of prisoners and consult their gods by means of human entrails.'

Such remarks have to be taken in their context: Tacitus was writing in the wake of the Roman Conquest and may well have wished to demonize the Druids as a means of justifying the invasion. But plenty of evidence for human sacrifice has come to light. At Danebury (see p. 217), for example, several skeletons were discovered at the bottom of large pits into which the bodies had been thrown with little decorum or ceremony. Also in Danebury was unearthed the pelvis of a male, hacked off at the thighs in what appeared to be a ritual sacrifice.

Similarly gruesome depositions have been found at other locations around the country, notably marshes: among the most famous is 'Lindlow Man', a remarkably well-preserved body of a male in his mid-twenties discovered in a peat bog near Wilmslow in Cheshire. After a final meal of bread, the individual had been struck over the head, strangled and had his throat cut before being committed to the mud.

While it is difficult to interpret the beliefs motivating such practices with absolute certainty, the wealth of material consigned to the earth in hillforts indicates that people revered deities who resided in the ground and that leaving gifts in pits was regarded as a way of communicating with them. Seed grain was stored in circular holes (while grain for eating was kept in stilted granaries above ground), and such pits were often found to contain offerings of food, or the bodies of whole animals such as horses and dogs.

The deposition of metal weapons and jewelry is a practice most closely associated with the Bronze Age, but it too continued on a smaller scale into the first century BC. Large hoards, some containing gold torcs and huge quantities of silver, have been found at sites such as Snettisham in Norfolk, which may, two thousand or more years ago, have been sacred groves.

It is also clear that certain lakes, marshes and stretches of rivers were also held as sacred. Some of the finest parade armour from the Iron Age was dredged from the Thames in London, while a shallow lake in Anglesey known as Llyn Cerrig Bach has yielded nearly two hundred metal items, including slave chains, swords, spearheads, fragments of shields, cauldrons, wagon tyres and horse gear.

Towards the end of the Iron Age, and into the Romano-British period, more formal shrines were also in use. Large hillforts, such as Danebury and Maiden Castle, have been found to hold prominent buildings at their centre, interpreted by archaeologists as religious or cult structures. Bigger temple complexes, enclosed within expansive rectangular or square palisades, have also been identified, one of the largest at them at in Suffolk (now beneath an industrial estate on the outskirts of Thetford). Another important shrine that remained in use well into the Roman period was the hot springs in Bath, dedicated to the goddess Sulis, whom the Romans converted into a hybrid deity, Sulis-Minerva.

Chesters Hill Fort, East Lothian

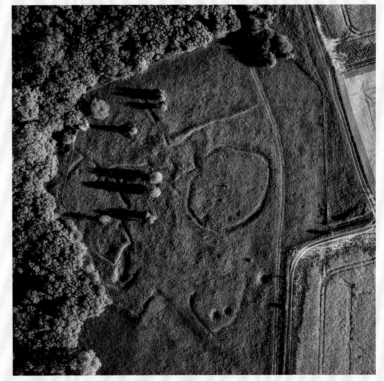

Rotherley Down, Wiltshire

191

Chalbury Dorset

British people take hillforts rather in their stride. They are ubiquitous across much of the country, and only the largest tend to attract much attention. Yet their appearance in the landscape midway through the first millennium BC marks a hugely significant moment in the evolution of prehistoric society.

Prior to this time, the majority of Britons lived as their forebears had done for at least two thousand years: in small, extended-family farmsteads, often with low walls enclosing a collection of roundhouses, byres, granaries and livestock pens. Then, in the sixth century BC, something changed to radically alter the complexion of life. We don't know for certain what it was – whether a threat or something else – but it must have been serious, because within decades a huge swathe of the population had shifted their dwellings to higher, more easily defensible ground and reinforced these communal settlements with earth ditches and palisaded ramparts.

Chalbury, overlooking Weymouth Bay and Portland Bill on the Dorset Coast, exemplifies the scale and nature of these early hillforts and the type of locations that were typically chosen for them.

Rather than the availability of water and easy access to cultivated land, the main attraction of the site was the steepness of the ground surrounding it. Ramparts were built around the hilltop and wooden stockades erected on them, providing clear lines of fire for defenders whose principal weapon would have been slings, using flint pebbles from nearby Chesil Beach as shot, along with bows and arrows.

The footprints of around thirty hut circles were identified at Chalbury when the site was investigated by archaeologists just before World War II, most of them around the enclosure's perimeter. Purbeck limestone extracted from ditches was used to strengthen the sloping embankments below the walls. One of the ditches was found to contain an 'urn field' cemetery holding around one hundred cremations in terracotta pots.

Reminders of previous, seemingly more peaceful eras rise from the Dorset Ridgeway to the north, where a row of enormous Early Bronze Age burial mounds dominates the horizon. These barrows are tricky to photograph from the air because they are surrounded by high-voltage electricity cables, but their presence lends an ancient feel to this chalk landscape.

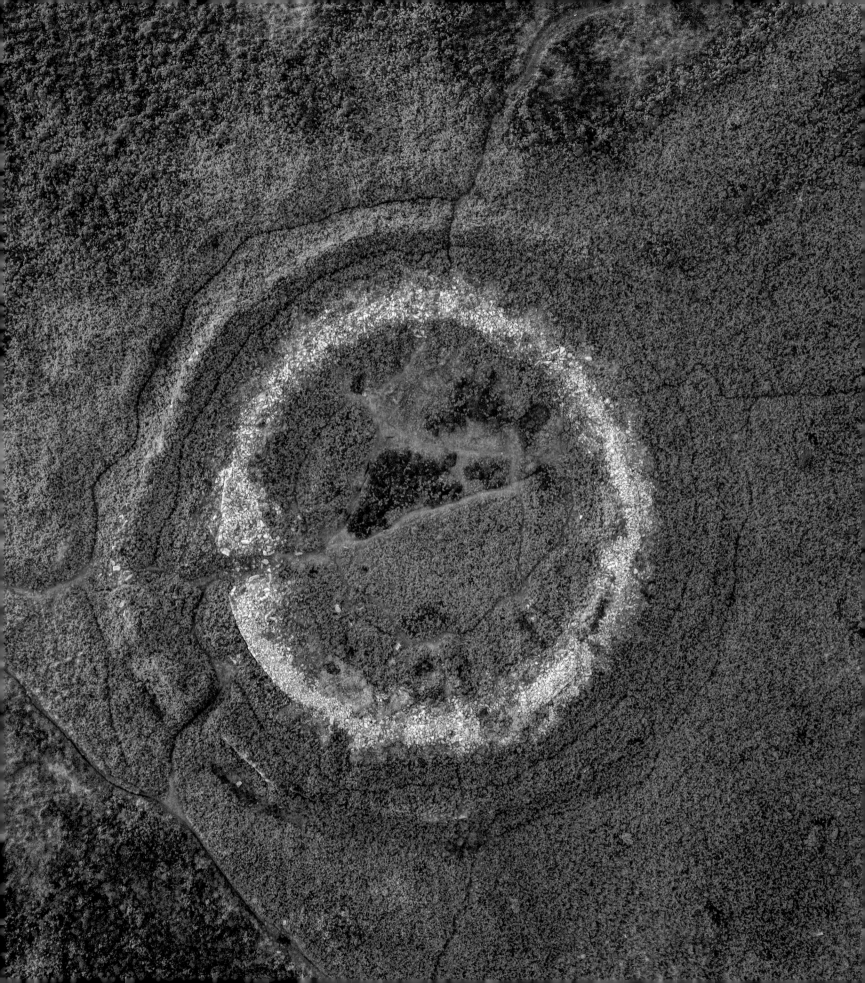

Chûn Castle West Penwith, Cornwall

High on the moors above Penzance in the far west of Cornwall, Chûn Castle is a classic example of the kind of hillfort that predominated in the southwest of Britain. Classified as a 'ring fort' by archaeologists, it dates from the late sixth century and consists of two concentric ramparts separated by a deep ditch, with a single entrance facing the winter solstice sunset.

Originally, the walls would have been four times the size they are now. In the nineteenth century, the land it stands on was auctioned and the freehold included rights to remove Chûn's stone; much of the Iron Age granite was removed to build Penanze and Madron.

Archaeological digs uncovered considerable quantities of pottery dating as far back as the early fourth century BC, most of it originating in Armorica (Brittany), with which this extremity of Cornwall enjoyed active trade links throughout prehistory.

The derelict chimneys and wheelhouses of old mines on the nearby coast hint at what the major export from here would have been: for thousands of years this was one of Europe's principal sources of tin and Chûn Castle would probably have been constructed to protect both the local population and the ingots they produced. The surrounding heathland is also littered with remnants from the pre-metal era, foremost among them Chûn Quoit (see p. 62), one of Cornwall's most impressive Neolithic dolmens.

Castle Dore Fowey, Cornwall

Another well-preserved Cornish ring fort is to be found on the high ground above the port and holiday resort of Fowey, in the southeast of the county. Castle Dore comprises a roughly circular ditch-and-bank enclosure with a fortified gateway on its northeast side, constructed in the fifth century BC. Around this, a second rampart was created at a slightly later date. Both would originally have bristled with hardwood palisades.

Rather than accommodating a community, this rather diminutive hillfort would have served as the seat of a clan chief, his extended family, their animals and grain stores – much as stone castles did in the medieval era. The wealth and power of the resident dynasty must in part have derived from trade passing through the port at the river mouth below. Fowey has one of the deepest and best-sheltered harbours in Britain and during the Iron Age would have been home to a fleet of boats carrying tin, copper, hides and other produce as cabotage trade along the south coast, as well as across the Channel to Armorica (Brittany). From the Saxon period, it also served as an embarkation point for pilgrims bound for Santiago de Compostela in Spain.

Today, the site is rather neglected, though it remains an obligatory destination for local school children and their teachers on history field trips. It is worth a visit for the views alone, which extend far out to sea and north to the tors of southeast Bodmin.

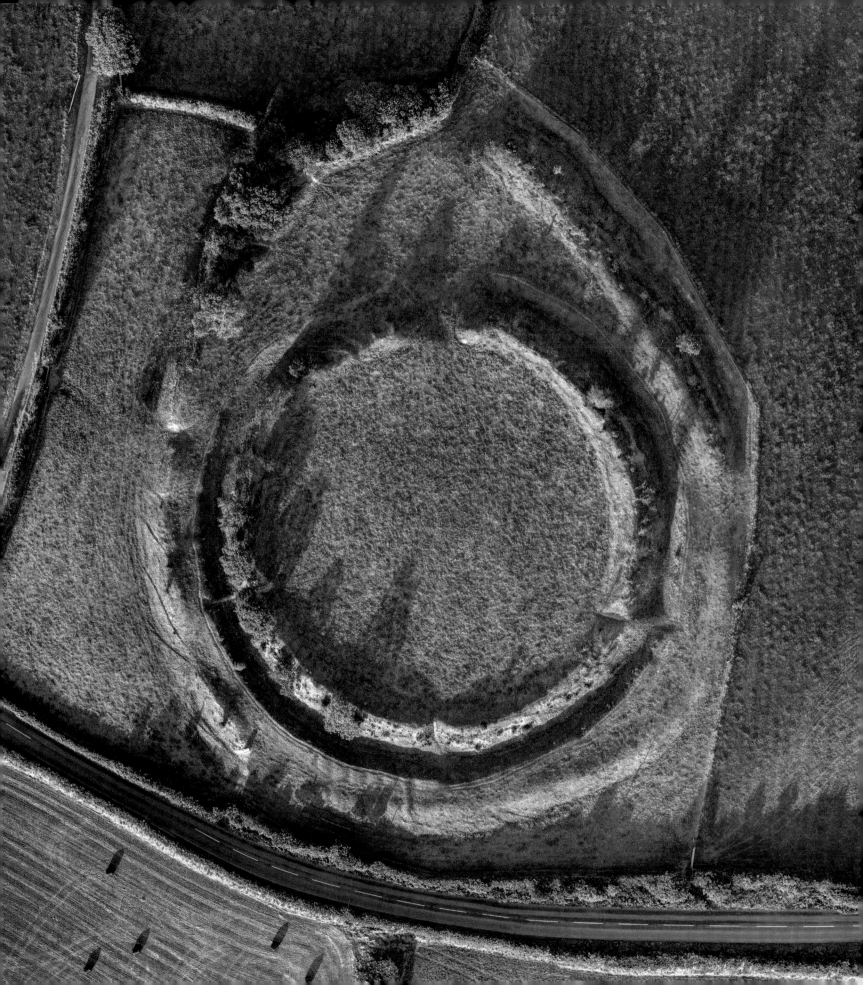

Clovelly Dykes North Devon

Enfolded by several oddly shaped ramparts, this Iron Age fort near the tiny port of Clovelly in northeast Devon is something of an enigma. No significant archaeological work has been carried out on it, so a firm chronology is lacking. But the presence inside its walls of Bronze Age flint scatters suggest the site was in use far back in prehistory.

Opinion is divided over whether the unusual layout, featuring five layers of enclosure, was intended to accommodate animals – perhaps during an annual livestock fair – or a fully fledged settlement. But the low height of the walls and absence of deep ditches suggest its purpose may not have been primarily defensive.

One plausible theory is that this may have been a hub for maritime trade in the Iron Age. Tin and silver ingots from mines on Dartmoor to the southwest have turned up along this stretch of coast overlooking the Bristol Channel, as well as pottery fragments bearing traces of olives and wine from the Mediterranean. Boats from here would also have been making regular crossings to Lundy Island, visible on the horizon, and beyond to Wales and Ireland.

Barely distinguishable at ground level, the site today is a total backwater, though in fine weather between Atlantic storms, the vivid blue of the sea, lush green pasture and concentric outlines of the old fort create an evocative spectacle.

Hengistbury Head Christchurch, Dorset

The pre-eminent port on the southwest coast of Britain for much of the Iron Age was Hengistbury Head, a sandy promontory forming the southern edge of Christchurch Harbour. From here, a thriving trade in goods drawn from the centre and west of Britain was carried out with Armorica (Brittany) and Normandy, from where luxury goods from Roman Gaul and the Mediterranean were imported.

Backed by a long, low hill, Hengistbury would have visible to prehistoric mariners from far out to sea, and the lagoon beyond, lined by gently shelving gravel beaches, offered a safe anchorage for wooden boats. The harbour had the additional advantage of lying at the mouth of two important rivers – the Wiltshire Avon, which extended north to Salisbury Plain, and the Stour, originating at western extremity of the Wessex chalklands. By means of these, goods could be transported far inland to Old Sarum (see p. 229) and other major hillforts lining the river routes.

Extensive archaeological work has been carried out at the site, notably by Barry Cunliffe, who identified layers of occupation dating back to the Neolithic. But it was Hengistbury's Iron Age settlement, bounded in the west by two deep earth ditches and ramparts (visible in the photograph), that yielded the most revealing finds.

These included tin, copper and silver from Dartmoor and West Cornwall, and lead from the Mendips, which were reconstituted and worked here for export. Armlets made from shale quarried at Kimmeridge, further west, along with corn and cattle from Hampshire to the north were also shipped through the port, probably along with 'hides, and slaves and dogs that are by nature suited to the purposes of the chase', as the Greek historian Strabo noted at the time.

The wealth of Armorican pottery and coins unearthed at Hengistbury suggests that the ports of northern Brittany were its main trading partners. This commerce, however, appears to have been adversely affected by the Gallic Wars of the mid-first century BC, when Julius Caesar's legions devastated Armorica. Thereafter, most trade to and from the south coast of Britain was conducted through hubs further southeast.

Cadbury Castle South Cadbury, Somerset

Evidence of cereal cultivation and livestock husbandry dating back to the Early Neolithic have been unearthed on the top of Cadbury Castle, in the Somerset Levels. But the standout find here – a magnificent shield of the 'Yetholm' type, reliably dated to around 1200 BC – derives from the Late Bronze Age. Featuring concentric ridges and rings of punch-marked (repoussé) tin-bronze, this exquisite object – which is believed to have been manufactured locally – was placed face down in the earth when still new and untarnished, probably as an offering to the chthonic deities. Pieces of the weapons that were used to pierce it were found in the soil directly below. The shield is now on display in the Museum of Somerset, Taunton.

Ploughing ceased on the hilltop early in the Middle Iron Age, when it was fortified with a stone enclosure. More elaborate defences appeared over the following centuries, taking their final form in the Late Iron Age, by which time Cadbury had grown into an oppidum-style settlement with a large number of roundhouses, workshops and shrines.

Archaeological digs conducted in the 1960s revealed evidence of burning and violent conflict around the main southwest gate, which is generally believed to date from the AD 40s, when the hillfort is likely to have been one of those besieged by the Second Legion under Vespasian.

In the late fifth century AD, after the Romans had decamped, the fort was occupied by a powerful local warlord who would almost certainly have resisted early Saxon incursions in the area and may have participated in the Battle of Badon (aka the Battle of Mons Badonicus), which forestalled the Germanic advance for at least a century. The battle was later associated with the figure of 'Arthur', mentioned by Bede and Nennius, hence Cadbury's long-standing identification as one of the mostly likely candidates for the site of the Camelot of Arthurian legend.

Traprain Law East Lothian

The Scottish equivalent of Cadbury Castle (see previous spread) surges from the Lothian plains around half an hour's drive east of Edinburgh, near the town of Haddington. An intrusion of volcanic magma, the landform was sculpted smooth through the Ice Age and its whaleback summit plateau provided the perfect site for a hillfort. Evidence of occupation dating from the Late Bronze Age until the twilight of the Roman Empire has been unearthed on the site.

The ramparts were enlarged and elaborated over several centuries during the Iron Age, when they enclosed one of largest oppida of the era, believed to have been the stronghold of the Votadini tribe. The Votadini were the principal power on the Lothian Plain during the Roman occupation, when the region lay between Hadrian's Wall and the Antonine Wall. Once the latter had been abandoned in AD 162, the tribe's territory became a buffer zone and this may explain an extraordinary find made on the hill.

During a dig on Traprain Law in 1919, archaeologists discovered a huge quantity of silver dating from the end of the Roman period. Comprising nearly three hundred fragments with a total weight of 24 kilograms (53 pounds), the hoard was mostly made up of aristocratic tableware that had been crumpled and hacked into pieces. The most plausible explanation is that the treasure was some kind of diplomatic payment to the Votadini for repelling the Picts, Scots and Angles who regularly raided the area when Roman power was on the wane (though it could equally have been booty from a Votadini raid south of Hadrian's Wall).

Whatever its origins, the silver was buried sometime in the mid-fifth century – whether as an offering to the gods or to hide it from attackers is unclear. Many of the fragments have been painstakingly reassembled and the resulting plates, flagons, drinking cups, coins and cutlery – all exquisitely decorated – now form a show-stopping display at the National Museum of Scotland.

The Brown and White Caterthuns Angus

Two of Britain's most striking prehistoric forts face each other from opposing hilltops above cloud-swept Strathmore, in the northeast Highlands of Scotland. Little is known about the Caterthuns beyond the fact both were constructed in the first half of the first millennium BC – the Early to Middle Iron Age.

Of the pair, the boat-shaped 'White Caterthun' is the most conspicuous. Evidence of occupation has been discovered within its pale-grey ramparts, which show signs of having been vitrified – a process by which stones are fused together by the application of extreme heat. Given the temperatures required to achieve this, the burning had to be intentional and carefully managed. The phenomenon, which occurs at numerous forts across Scotland, has traditionally been interpreted as an attempt to strengthen the walls, but it actually weakens them. A more likely explanation is that the firing was some kind of decommissioning ritual, undertaken

by its inhabitants when the fort was deserted, or in the wake of an attack.

Unlike its neighbour, the 'Brown Caterthun', on the more northerly of the two hills, does not appear to have been inhabited. Curious spoke-like paths radiate out from its concentric walls via a series of openings, but what purpose they served remains obscure. The best guess is that the structure served as some kind of ceremonial or cult centre for the inhabitants of the 'white' hillfort.

The mystery surrounding these survivors from Scotland's distant past only adds to their allure. Set amid the foothills of the Cairngorm mountains, whose dark purple grouse moors rise sheer from the far side of Strathmore, the Caterthuns look like vestiges from some epic Iron Age encounter between rival Pictish clans, or a location from a *Game of Thrones*-style drama.

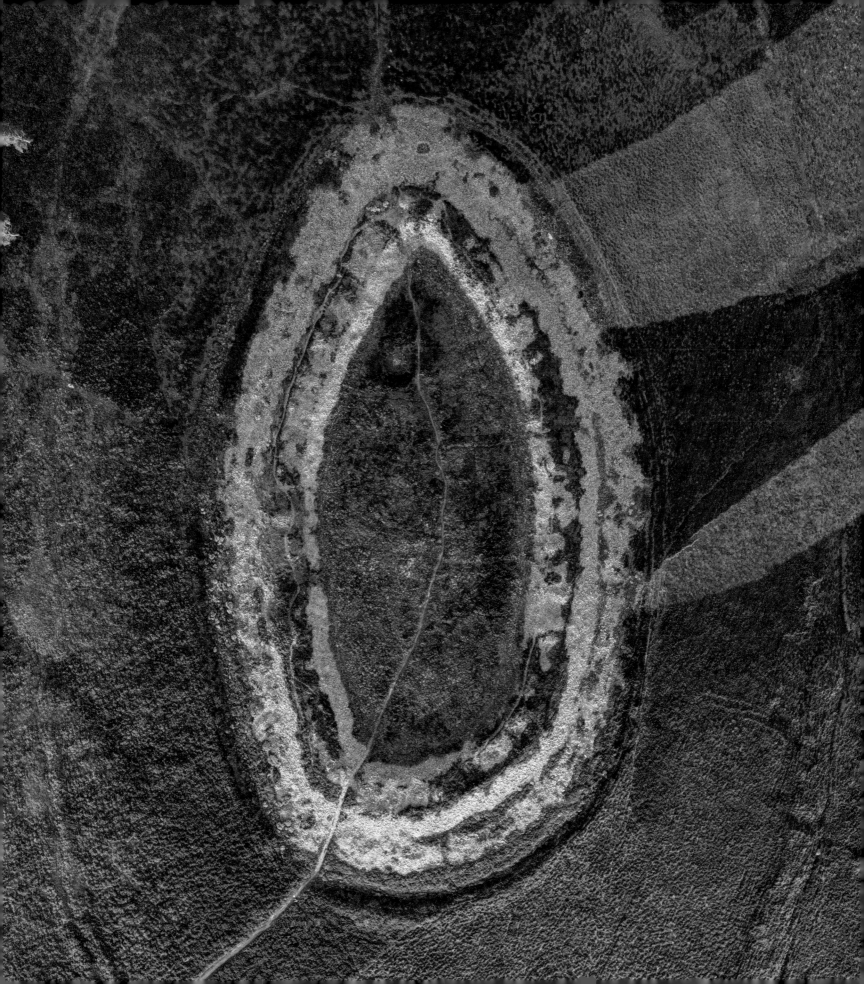

Dun Beag Isle of Skye

Fortified, bottle-shaped towers, brochs, are a familiar sight across the Hebrides, Orkney Islands, Shetlands and far north of the Scottish mainland, where they rise – generally in a ruinous state – from exposed clifftops and knolls. They are the region's most visible vestiges from the Late Iron Age, although little is known about the people who built them or why they were constructed.

The traditional explanation is that they were early versions of 'stately homes' designed to project power and prestige. But the large number of them and the fact that many occur in close proximity suggest they may have been more humble in nature – farmer-herder dwellings that were designed both to be lived in and to repulse attacks.

Some credence to this is lent by the '*torri*' erected by the Genoese around their Mediterranean territory in the eighteenth century. While besieging one in Corsica, Nelson was so impressed by how effectively a tiny number of defenders were able to withstand bombardment and musket fire from his gunships that he ordered a string of similar structures, nicknamed 'martello towers', to be erected along the south coast of Britain as a front-line defence against Napoleon's navy.

Indeed, theories about the purpose of brochs suggest they may have formed a kind of early warning system of lookout posts intended to alert local populations that a raid was imminent.

Ranging from 5 to 15 metres (17 to 50 feet) wide and 11 to 13 metres (36 to 43 feet) tall, most were circular and empty at ground level, with floors inserted higher up accessed via spiral staircases. They were probably roofed with timber and conical thatch. While some were sited close to water and fields, others were raised on much wilder terrain.

This is the case with Dun Beag, one of the best-preserved brochs on the Isle of Skye, which crowns a rocky bluff surveying the vast sweep of tundra and crofting settlements around Loch Bracadale, on the island's northwest coast.

Archaeological investigations carried out at Dun Beag in 1914 and 1920 yielded finds of stone tools, a gold ring and various bronze objects, along with hundreds of glass beads and coins suggesting the broch may have been occupied into the Georgian era.

The Broch of Gurness Orkney

Dating from the Middle Iron Age, between 500 and 200 BC, the Broch of Gurness on the north coast of the Orkney mainland presided, unlike Dun Beag (see previous spread), over a small hamlet. The vestiges of a boundary ditch and bank roughly 45 metres (148 feet) across encircles the ruined tower, inside which the remnants of numerous drystone houses, livestock pens and sheds have been unearthed. The broch appears to have been abandoned sometime around 100 BC, when the ditch was filled in, after which the site was used as a farmstead until the eighth century.

Human remains and shield fragments of Viking origin discovered nearby suggest the headland was later settled, or used as a funerary site, by Norse incomers. It is not hard to see why: the setting, looking across the vivid blue waters of Eynhallow Sound to the Island of Rousay, is spellbinding.

The Sound would have been an important resource during the Iron Age. Archaeological work has revealed that cod, seal and whale meat formed part of the local diet, while skins from marine mammals would have provided furs for clothing and bedding.

In the houses grouped around the broch survive the remnants of hearths, sleeping spaces and stone cupboards reminiscent of those in use at the Neolithic settlement at Skara Brae on the Orkney mainland.

Cissbury Ring Worthing, West Sussex

At the opposite end of the country from Orkney (see previous spread), Cissbury Ring exemplifies the vastly different ways of life being lived by people at the extremities of Britain during the Iron Age. The ramparts of the hillfort enclose a huge area of 26 hectares (64 acres), making this the second-largest settlement of its type in Britain and one of the biggest anywhere in Europe. The walls are believed to have been built in the Middle Iron Age, around 250 BC, and remained in use until shortly after the Roman conquest of the 40s AD.

The most interesting discoveries here from the Iron Age were a number of pits dug 4 metres (13 feet) beneath the inner ditch at the northeast edge of the fort, in which an extraordinary array of objects had been placed, from everyday items such as unbroken loom weights, knives and fragments of Middle Iron Age pottery to vitrified clay bricks, 404 pebbles (used in slingshots), pieces of a bronze scabbard, animal bones and oyster shells. The most likely explanation is that this was some kind of ritual deposition rather than a midden, but what determined the choice of contents remains a mystery.

Aside from its formidable size, Cissbury's other claim to fame is the presence, on its western side, of an extensive Neolithic flint mine. Second only in scale to the one at Grime's Graves in Norfolk (see p. 77), the complex comprised 270 shafts extending from between 3 and 36 metres (10 and 118 feet) underground. Many of them were too narrow to be accessible by adults, and were propped up by slender pillars that were clearly fragile: during archaeological digs, several human skeletons were found in the subterranean labyrinth, some of them carefully laid to rest with the bones of animals such as otters, roe deer, pigs, oxen, goats and foxes.

Danebury Stockbridge, Hampshire

No Iron Age hillfort in Britain has been as comprehensively studied as Danebury in Hampshire. Between 1969 and 1988, ahead of its conversion for use as a country park by the county council, archaeologist Barry Cunliffe and his team spent twenty seasons investigating the various phases of development of the fort; how its inhabitants lived; and the relationship between Danebury and other settlements in the area.

Dating from the mid-fifth century BC, the first structure on this low hill near the Test Valley consisted of a single earth-and-ditch rampart with two entrances on opposing sides. These walls were enlarged and added to on several occasions over the succeeding centuries, and a more heavily fortified gateway constructed on the east side.

The archaeologists were able to identify a large number of wattle and timber roundhouses (and some with wooden plank walls) in the fort's interior, along with the remains of grain storage pits, stilted granaries and rectangular buildings believed to have been shrines. It became clear that the economy of the hillfort revolved primarily around sheep and corn, supplemented with metalworking and various crafts, such as the manufacture of polished stone armlets made using shale imported from Kimmeridge on the Dorset coast.

At its peak, Danebury's population is estimated to have been around 200–350. Like many other sites in the region, the stronghold was abandoned around 100 BC after what appears to have been an attack on a large scale, during which the east gate was burned down. Around one hundred bodies dating from this time were discovered in a charnel pit, many of them bearing signs of injuries consistent with wounds from swords, spears and slingshots.

One of the most fascinating discoveries by Cunliffe's team was the numerous objects unearthed at the bottom of grain storage pits inside the fort. Ranging from horse and other animal carcasses to human skeletons, hides, bales of wood, pots of cheese and even a meteorite, these were interpreted as ritual offerings to the gods of the underworld, perhaps made to ensure the fertility of seed grain or as thanks for a successful harvest.

Maiden Castle Dorchester, Dorset

Rising from the lush valley on the south side of Dorchester like a giant green galleon, Maiden Castle is a hillfort of superlatives, with the most imposing ramparts, the deepest ditches, the biggest enclosed area and longest history of use of any comparable structure in Europe.

The hilltop was first fortified in the Early Iron Age, around 600 BC, by a single rampart encircling a Neolithic causeway carved more than three thousand years earlier. Around 450 BC, the fort tripled in size and gained four rows of concentric ramparts on its southern side and three on its northern flank. The gateways were also upgraded, becoming complex mazes designed to confuse and trap would-be attackers.

After Tessa Verney Wheeler and her husband, Mortimer, conducted excavations here in the 1930s, they concluded that Maiden Castle had borne the brunt of the Claudian invasion of AD 43–47, citing as evidence a 'war grave' discovered at the eastern gateway, which contained skeletons bearing traces of a violent death. Subsequent investigations, however, have cast doubt on this narrative: the burnt-out layer discovered nearby is now known to have been residue from an iron workshop, while the 'ballistra bolts', allegedly from a Roman catapult, were of British origin.

By the end of the first century BC, the west end of Maiden Castle had been largely abandoned. Settlement from this time became concentrated in the eastern half, spilling around the gateway. Bisecting the fort was a track leading to a circular building in its centre, interpreted as some kind of shrine.

Following the conquest, the site fell into disuse after Durnovaria (Dorchester), a Roman garrison and market town, was founded on the hill to the north.

Abbotsbury Dorset

Little is known about the history or inhabitants of this diminutive hillfort on the South Dorset Ridgeway, beyond the fact it must, at the very end of the Iron Age, have been one of the strongholds of the Durotriges tribe, who famously resisted the advance of Vespasian's Second Legion in the 40s AD. It is therefore likely that the site was besieged before or after any attack on nearby Maiden Castle (see previous spread), though no evidence for this has ever been uncovered.

The footprints of numerous roundhouses cluster on the fort's east side, surrounded by ditches designed to keep the hut floors dry and prevent their daub walls from rotting. As was the custom, the doorways would have been aligned with the midwinter solstice sunrise and the view from them no less wonderful than it is today, extending across the great sweep of Chesil Beach to Portland Bill, and west over Lyme Bay to the shadowy coastline of South Devon, receding into the distance.

From this vantage point, Abbotsbury's occupants would have had a grandstand view of the ships sailing between Hengistbury Head (see p. 201) and Armorica (Brittany). This maritime trade route was the source of the region's prosperity and when it became severed midway through the first century BC, following Julius Caesar's attack on the Armorican tribes, the region suffered. Coins minted by the Durotriges in the wake of the Gallic War became increasingly debased, while those produced in the southeast of England contained higher quantities of gold and silver, reflecting the political shift that gathered momentum in the decades leading up to the Roman invasion of AD 43.

Badbury Rings Dorset

Another Durotriges stronghold, this spectacular hillfort is the fifth in a series of six that were established along the course of the Stour Valley in the Late Iron Age. The fortresses commanded the main river route northwest towards the mines of Mendip Plateau, whose lead-silver alloy was among the region's major exports in the first century BC. From Badbury, the Stour flows on to Christchurch Harbour, where Hengistbury Head (see p. 201) served the region's principal metalworking centre and port.

Badbury is also less than half a day's walk from Poole Harbour to the south – another busy port at this time. Two sizeable jetties dating from the late second century BC have been discovered on Green Island, and these would have provided access to deep water channels by means of which ships could enter and leave the lagoon. From there, the River Frome meandered west to Maiden Castle (see p. 218), deep in Durotriges territory: salt, grain, lead and Kimmeridge shale, used to make polished black-stone armlets and rings, were the main exports. Amphorae of a type originating in Pompeii and Calabria, used to transport wine, have been unearthed in the settlement opposite Green Island, along with substantial quantities of Armorican coins, proving that maritime trade with the coast of northern France thrived here in the Late Iron Age.

The three concentric ramparts of Badbury give the impression of a sizeable village, but archaeological work carried out in 1998 only identified twenty-eight possible hut circles on the site. A desire to project power and status is often given as an explanation for such disproportionately large defences, but sites like this would also have been used to store seed grain and other essentials for farmsteads and hamlets dispersed across a wide area, and would thus have been of great importance.

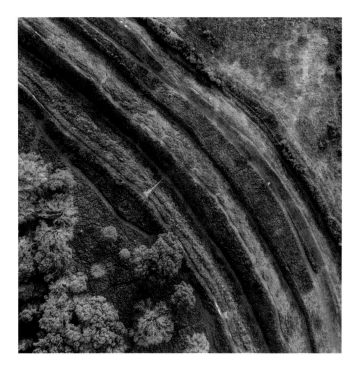

Eggardon Hill Dorset

Draped across a slender chalk spur above the Mangerton Valley near Bridport, Eggardon dominates the rolling hinterland that rises from behind Chesil Beach. The hilltop boasts arguably the best view of any Iron Age fort in the region, taking in a huge sweep of downland and coast.

No archaeological work has ever been carried out at the site, but it must have been one of the main strongholds of the Durotriges tribe, with connections to Maiden Castle (see p. 218) in the east, Chilcombe Hill to the south, and Pilsdon Pen to the northwest. This would have been the region's heartland, encompassing fertile pasture for grain cultivation in the valleys, good grazing on the downs and easy access to dependable fishing in Lyme Bay.

Eggardon loaned its name to a fictious moorland – Egdon Heath – that featured prominently in the novels of Thomas Hardy, including *Tess of the D'Urbervilles* and *The Mayor of Casterbridge*. The hill, however, is more closely associated with the figure of Isaac Gulliver, an infamous local smuggler whose gang of fifteen 'luggers' dominated the illegal trade in liquor, lace and tea from the Continent in the Georgian era. Gulliver planted a hexagonal coppice of trees on the hilltop which his sailors used to navigate by; the plantation was removed by the King's excisemen, but the outline of the hexagon survives and can clearly been seen from the air.

Hod Hill Dorset

Maiden Castle (see p. 218) may be the 'poster-child' Iron Age hillfort in Dorset, but this less well-known one in the Stour Valley must, judging by its scale and imposing defences, have been of comparable importance. Geophysical surveys identified the footprints of around two hundred roundhouses, hearths and storage pits crammed into the site, mostly dating from the third and second centuries BC.

Since Tessa and Mortimer Wheeler first promulgated the idea in the 1930s, hillforts in this region were thought to have bucked the trend of the late first century BC by becoming more densely populated at a time when others were falling into disuse. Archaeological work carried out in the late 1990s, however, has cast some doubt on this assertion. Hod Hill's ramparts now appear to have fallen into disrepair through the years leading up to the Claudian conquest of AD 43, and the settlement reduced rather than grew.

Clusters of ballista bolts concentrated in one area of the fort, where previously there had been a large roundhouse, were for years interpreted as proof that the stronghold had been attacked by the Second Augustan Legion on its way northwest: the roundhouse was thought to have been a 'chief's residence' on which the besiegers had trained their fire. But a more plausible and prosaic explanation is that they ended up there in the course of target practice by soldiers garrisoned at the square fort the Romans erected in the northwest corner of the hillfort, where the foundation platforms of ballista catapults have been reliably identified.

Overlooking the Stour Valley, this military outpost will have been sited on the hilltop as an 'observe and control' centre, allowing the Roman authorities to oversee the Mendip lead trade, which passed via the river below to the Solent region.

A no less spectacular hillfort with magnificent views over the Blackmore Vale may be explored a few miles west of Hod at Hambledon Hill.

Old Sarum Salisbury, Wiltshire

A centre of power for over two and a half thousand years, Old Sarum owes its prominence to its position overlooking a wide plain, surrounded by rolling downland, where four rivers intersect. From this hilltop, whose flanks were sculpted and fortified with giant ramparts in the fourth century BC (the Middle Iron Age), the region's chiefs and kings and their forces could control trade and the movement of people between the Wessex chalklands and the coast.

At the time of the Claudian invasion, the site is known to have been a stronghold of the Atrebates, a tribe founded by the fugitive Gallo-Belgic chief Commius, who had been an ally of Caesar's during the Roman incursions of the 50s BC but who later allied himself with Vercingetorix, chief of the Gauls, in his revolt against Rome. However, when the Gauls were defeated by Caesar in the Battle of Alesia (in

the Bourgogne region of France) in AD 52, Commius fled to Britain to join members of his own tribe who had already settled around the Solent area, and formed a new capital at Calleva Atrebatum (Silchester, in modern-day Hampshire).

It appears that Commius's son, Verica, later made peace with Rome and ruled as a client king until he was overthrown by Caratacus, chief of the Catuvellauni tribe, in AD 43 – an event Emperor Claudius famously used as a 'casus belli' to justify his invasion of Britain the following year.

The ditches and banks of the old Iron Age ramparts were made use of by William the Conqueror in the early eleventh century. Old Sarum is allegedly where he was first presented with the Domesday Book. From the air, the outlines of the old Norman cathedral and motte-and-bailey castle can clearly be seen, encircled by the great Iron Age ramparts.

Figsbury Ring Wiltshire

On high ground above the Bourne Valley to the east of Old Sarum (see previous spread), another Atrebates hillfort dominates the southern approach to Salisbury Plain. Figsbury Ring, like the other Iron Age strongholds in this area, is circular in plan, with two concentric ramparts enfolding the central area where the roundhouses and granaries were located. Between them lies a 30-metre (98-foot) wide expanse of level ground – an unusual feature for this type of fort that has intrigued archaeologists for decades.

The most plausible explanation for the anomaly is that the inner circuit may have originally been a much older enclosure that was subsequently strengthened. No one, however, suspected just how much older it might have been until pieces of Grooved Ware pottery came to light in digs during the 1980s, pointing towards Early Neolithic origins. Could this have been a causewayed enclosure, or a seasonal livestock camp? Geophysical surveys have proved inconclusive, though discoveries of flint scatters dating from the Mesolithic suggest the hilltop has been a centre of occupation for many thousands of years.

Yarnbury Camp Wiltshire

A few miles from Stonehenge (see p. 110) on the southern side of Salisbury Plain, Yarnbury Camp retains traces of two Iron Age hillforts. The first dates from fourth century BC and is now just visible as a shallow ditch. This smaller, older camp was encircled two hundred years later by the triple-layered ramparts of a considerably larger one, whose approach was fortified by a wonderfully convoluted gateway on its southeast side. The footprints of over 130 structures have been detected within its walls, ranging from 7 to 15 metres (23 to 50 feet) in diameter, spanning a long period of occupation. Clearly, the size and status of this community increased greatly between the Middle and Late Iron Age.

An extensive Romano-British field system, with its roots in earlier eras, has been identified around the hillfort, which, long after it was deserted, became the venue of the Yarnborough Sheep Fair. Held in October each year, the event attracted shepherds, stall holders and daytrippers from across the region until it was moved to a more convenient site in the Wylye Valley in 1919.

Today, Yarnbury lies on private land and is not easily accessible from the adjacent A303. The grassy banks visible from the main road offer few clues as to the scale and magnificence of the site when viewed from the air.

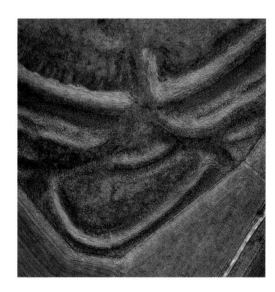

Forts of the North Wessex Scarp

The chalklands of Wessex extend from Dorset in the south to Sussex in the east, and north as far as Berkshire and Wiltshire. This whole area is rich in prehistoric remains, including, of course, the great Neolithic sites of Avebury and Stonehenge (see pp. 106 and 110). But it also holds many of Britain's most impressive hillforts. Dating from the Middle and Late Iron Age, the largest of these are to be found on the fringes of the chalk plateau, close to, or on, the scarp slopes that fall to the surrounding river valleys and plains.

The choice of location in each case invariably becomes apparent once you visit these ancient strongholds. With extensive views and protected from attack on two or three sides by steep hillsides, they stood on the most readily defensible land for miles, often within easy reach of important rivers.

The staggering scale of the bigger forts, however, is not easily explained. Whatever prompted the inhabitants of Iron Age Wessex to expend such a considerable collective effort one can only imagine: undoubtedly, the times when they were built – between the fourth and late second centuries BC – must have been unstable. What is sometimes described as 'the bow wave' of the Roman Empire's advance into Gaul

Scratchbury

Battlesbury

was starting to be felt, unsettling the old status quo and, evidently, leading to violent conflict in southern Britain.

The hillforts lying on the western and northern extremity of the chalklands were particularly heavily fortified, suggesting they may have presided over a frontier of sorts between long-forgotten tribal groups or confederacies.

The Warminster-Westbury Group

Three massive hillforts encrust the southwestern fringes of Salisbury Plain, overlooking the Wylye Valley near the Wiltshire market towns of Warmister and Westbury.

Scratchbury and Battlesbury, just outside Warminster, lie on land owned by the Ministry of Defence – part of the Imber artillery range – but are easily accessible. Their imposing ramparts and ditches date from the late second century BC and encompass prominent Early Bronze Age barrows excavated by William Cunnington and Richard Colt-Hoare in the early nineteenth century. The finds, including amber jewellery, jadeite axes and decorated terracotta urns from Beaker burials, are displayed in Devizes Museum.

On a comparable scale, Bratton Camp, above Westbury, is best known for its white horse chalk figure, but the

Bratton

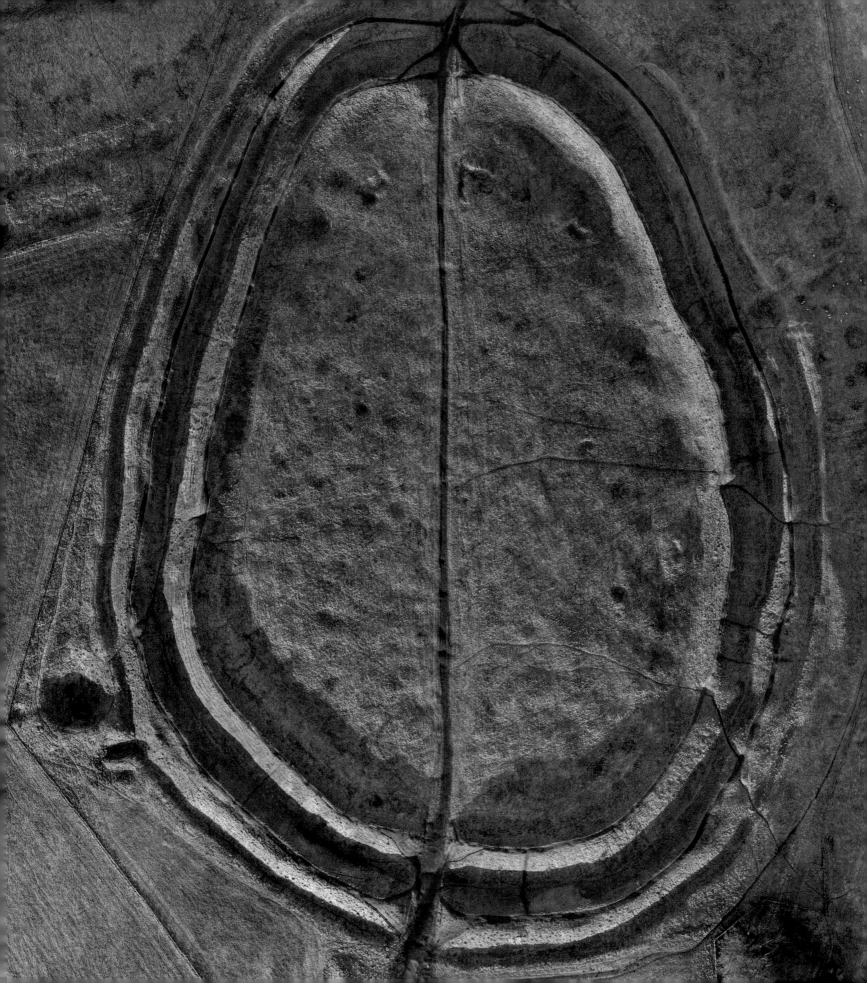

Uffington Castle

Liddington Castle

hillfort also holds an enormous Early Neolithic long barrow. Somewhere in the fields below it is the most likely site of the Battle of Edrington (or 'Ethandun') in which King Alfred of Saxon Wessex defeated the Danes under Guthrum in AD 873.

The Ridgeway Group

Another impressive chain of Late Iron Age hillforts lies along the Ridgeway, an ancient track skirting the northern limits of the chalklands.

Barbury Castle, to the south of Swindon, has two deep defensive ditches and ramparts forming a distinctive, symmetrical pear shape. Traces of numerous roundhouses and granaries that were once crammed inside it may clearly be seen from the air.

A few miles to the east along the Ridgeway in the Marlborough Downs, Liddington is believed to be one of the oldest hillforts in Britain. Pottery finds made here indicate occupation from the seventh until the fifth centuries BC, when the site was apparently deserted. Its oval earthworks, pierced by causewayed entrances on two sides, would originally have been surmounted by wood and stone palisades. A large pit discovered during archaeological work in the 1970s, measuring 1.5 metres (5 feet) in diameter and at least 2.4 metres (nearly 8 feet) deep, is believed to have been some kind of ritual shaft. Liddington's other claim to fame is that is the most likely site of the Battle of Badon (aka Mons Badonicus), in which the Saxons were defeated by a Brythonic army in the late sixth century AD, as chronicled by Gildas and Bede.

The site of Badon, however, could equally have been Uffington Castle, further east along the Ridgeway in Oxfordshire. Fortified with a timber box palisade and an inner ditch lined with diamond-hard sarsen stones, its ramparts offer a delightful walk in summer, when the grassy banks are speckled with harebells and yellow brimstone butterflies feasting on the buckthorn that grows prolifically in the area.

Warham Camp Norfolk

Warham Camp, in Norfolk, overlooks the banks of the River Stiffkey, around an hour's walk inland from the marshy north coast of East Anglia. In the Late Iron Age, this was the territory of the Iceni, a tribe about which comparatively little is known beyond the fact that their ruling elite had a penchant for very fancy metalwork. Numerous hoards of exquisitely decorated electrum torcs, arm rings and bronze horse tack have been discovered in the region, most famously at Snettisham.

Sumptuously adorned steeds pulling war chariots are likely to have been a common sight at Warham and the other Iceni strongholds further south, where the tribe's most illustrious daughter, Boudica, originated and from where she mounted her ill-fated insurrection against Roman rule in AD 60–61.

The rebellion, of course, ended badly for the British. Tacitus claims 80,000 Britons were massacred during the Roman reprisals, in the wake of which Boudica is said to have ended her life with poison.

Warham was originally enclosed by complete rings. Its southern gate, however, was demolished by the local landowner in the 1700s in order to strengthen the course of the river. Archaeologist Barry Cunliffe has suggested that its distinctive circular shape, a trait common to several hillforts in this area, may be a tradition dating back to the Late Bronze Age.

Today, the site is as tranquil a spot as you'll find in East Anglia, its grassy banks alive with butterflies and the air filled in early summer with the honking of geese grazing amid the nearby water meadows.

British Camp Malvern Hills

The ditches and counterscarps of two great hillforts, both dating from the Late Iron Age, sculpt the undulating ridgeline of the Malvern Hills: the first at Herefordshire Beacon; the second further south on Midsummer Hill. Thanks largely to the work lavished on it in medieval times, when a large castle was erected on its summit, the former is the better known of the pair, and the most spectacular from the air. Known as 'British Camp' today, it extends over three separate peaks that fall sharply to the Severn Vale on one side and the pretty, rolling hills and deciduous woods of Shropshire on the other.

The name 'Malvern' is believed to derive from the Brythonic 'moel bryn', meaning 'bare hill', and indeed, it is likely the tree cover that would have carpeted this serpent-like massif when the first farmers discovered it in the Early Neolithic was long gone by the Middle Bronze Age, when a series of cremation cemeteries were established on the high ridgetop.

Forming a shadowy presence between the rivers Severn and Wye, the Malverns are believed to have marked the line of an ancient border. Excavations of the Shire Ditch, a defensive earthwork dug along the summit ridge in 1207 by Gilbert de Claire, the Earl of Gloucester, have revealed the existence of much older banks beneath, thought to date from the Late Bronze Age.

By the time the first hillfort was created on Herefordshire Beacon in the third century BC, the old trackway that crossed the hills at near Wyche Cutting had become an important trade route. Carried by mule and donkey, salt extracted from pits beside the River Salwarpe in Droitwich, 32 kilometres (20 miles) to the northeast, was the principal commodity traded along this prehistoric track. Three hundred 'currency bars' unearthed in two holes discovered alongside it are believed to have been ritual depositions, giving some indication of the wealth that Iron Age trade must have brought to the region.

Crug Hywel Brecon Beacons, Powys

The Silures were a tribe who dominated the valleys and coastal plain of what is now southeast Wales in the century before Roman rule in Britain. With its drystone ramparts, pierced on their southeastern flank by a small, fortified gateway, this eagle's-nest hillfort, high above the Usk Valley, overlooking the town of Crickhowell (to which the site lent its name), is typical of the strongholds created in the Brecon Beacons to control trade through the region. Only a handful of dwellings have been identified within its walls, however it is likely that the population lived at more convenient sites lower down the mountainside, retreating to the high citadel only in times of danger.

The Silures were to prove a thorn in the side of the Romans after AD 43. Following the defeat of the powerful Catuvellauni tribe by Aulus Plautius's legions at the Battle of the River Medway (in Kent), their chief, Caratacus, fled west to join the Silures, leading the Welsh in a guerrilla-style resistance against Roman rule that lasted for eight years. Not until AD 78 were the Silures fully brought to heel, which Tacitus rather ambiguously claims was achieved 'neither by cruelty, nor by clemency'.

Either way, a large, rectangular oppidum was created for the inhabitants of Llanmelis hillfort, the most prominent stronghold in Silurian territory. Named 'Venta Silurum', the new settlement comprised an amphitheatre, shops, a forum, a temple, a baths complex and a military garrison. Large sections of its walls remain intact on the outskirts of modern Caerwent, 8 kilometres (5 miles) southwest of Chepstow – the best preserved of their kind in the country.

As well as chronicling Roman encounters with the tribe in the time of Caratacus, Tacitus also comments on the physical appearance of the Silures, famously referring to their 'swarthy faces' and the 'curly quality of their hair', which he attributed to distant Iberian origins – a hypothesis that modern archaeological data and DNA evidence suggests may have been correct.

Castell Dinas Talgarth, Powys

Presiding over one of the main breaches in the Black Mountains of Wales, Castell Dinas epitomizes the spirit of defiance for which its Iron Age inhabitants, the Silures, became renowned. The outlines of the prehistoric counterscarps and ditches and can still be clearly made out from the air, along with the remnants of the hillfort's original entrance on its north side (visible at the right extremity of the structure in the photograph).

The many lumps and bumps visible inside the ramparts are vestiges of a huge keep and great hall added in Norman times, most likely by William FitzOsbern, the first Earl of Hereford, who was a close associate of William the Conqueror and among only a few of his lords known to have been present at the Battle of Hastings.

FitzOsbern's incursion into the region four years later was prompted by a revolt by the Welsh princes, allied with the Saxon warlord Eadric the Wild. The rebellion was quashed and several castles built around the region to ensure the subjugation of its troublesome chiefs, among them the one at Castell Dinas.

Over the succeeding centuries, the site changed hands several times between the de Braose family, King John, the FitzHerberts and other regional power brokers until it was destroyed by Owain Glyndwr during the Welsh Revolt of the early fifteenth century. By the time the antiquarian John Leland visited the castle in 1538, it had been completely abandoned and lay in ruins.

Flanked by the bracken-covered spurs of Waun Fach (to the west) and Mynydd Troed to the east, Castell Dinas affords spectacular views down the Rhiangoll Valley to the south, and north towards the mountains of mid-Wales.

Pen y Crug Brecon, Powys

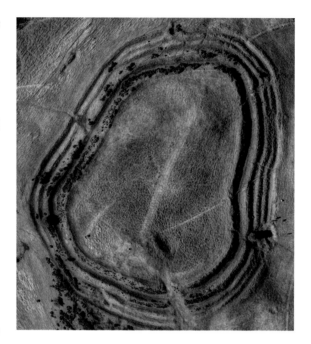

Few Iron Age strongholds in Britain command a view as dramatic as the one extending from the ramparts of Pen y Crug, near the town of Brecon in mid-Wales. Forming a wall of windswept Silurian sandstone, the high peaks of the Brecon Beacons range dominate the southern horizon, while the bracken-covered fells of Mynydd Epynt rise to the north. Between the two stretch the gentler slopes of the elegantly glaciated and elaborately pastured Usk Valley – a panorama that can have changed little since the first century BC, when this Welsh 'Shangri La' formed the northern limits of Silures territory.

The oval-shaped fort encloses the summit of the hill with a particularly impressive set of ramparts – the most elaborate of any in Wales. No less than five concentric layers fortify the citadel's north and east flanks (the top and right sides of the structure as you look at the photograph on the opposite page). On its southwest side, where the approach was steeper (bottom left), fewer layers of banks were required. The most interesting feature here though is the spot where the four ramparts on the northwest flank split to become five: a point more clearly visible from the air than the ground.

The explanation for such convoluted defences was probably the proximity, on the valley floor below, of the confluence of the Honddu and Usk rivers – a site valued throughout history for its strategic importance. After the defeat of the Silures by Sextus Julius Frontinus in AD 75, a Roman fort was built to the southwest of Pen y Crug, near the banks of the Usk, at a site known as Y Gaer. The stronghold (excavated by Mortimer Wheeler in the 1920s) was designed to accommodate around five hundred cavalrymen recruited from the ranks of the Vettones tribe of central Spain.

The Vettones, a notoriously militaristic band of Hispano-Celts, had allied with Hannibal and other adversaries of Rome to resist the legions, but after defeat at the hands of Julius Caesar in 61 BC, were incorporated into the Roman army, later playing a key role in the subjugation of Wales (an irony given the fact that they may well have shared a common ancestry with the Silures; see p. 242).

Caer Caradoc Church Stretton, Shropshire

Draped over a whaleback ridge overlooking the Stretton Gap in Shropshire, Caer Caradoc commands a superb view encompassing the Wrekin, the Malverns and distant Hay Bluff in the Black Mountains of Wales. The hill's natural outlines were exploited to great effect by the fort's builders in the Iron Age, who incorporated numerous basalt outcrops within the two ring banks they carved around the rim of the summit plateau. The ramparts on the south side (far left in the photograph below) were fortified by an additional ditch and wall, penetrated by a narrow entrance. No such measure was needed on the northern approach (featured in main photo), where a path wriggles up a much steeper incline.

The combined effect of the expansive panoramas and the craggy ramparts is dramatic, and may in part explain why the site has long been associated with one of the great resistance figures of the British Iron Age. Caratacus, leader of the Catuvellauni (from modern-day Essex), was the warlord whose attack on the Atrebates tribe, allied in the late first century with Rome, was used by Claudius as an excuse to invade Britain in AD 43.

Having been twice defeated by Aulus Plautius shortly after the invasion, Caratacus fled west into the territory of the Silures and Ordovices tribes in Wales, with whom he waged a guerrilla-style war against the Romans. The adventure came to an end in a desperate last stand at a hillfort described in detail by Tacitus. The Celts, he wrote, chose, 'a place for battle so that entry, exit, everything would be unfavourable to us and for the better to his own men, with steep mountains all around, and, wherever a gentle access was possible, he strewed rocks in front in the manner of a rampart'.

The precise location of the fort is a matter of debate, but Caer Caradoc is the site most often identified with the siege, which ended in another defeat for Caratacus. He escaped north to the territory of the Brigantes (in modern-day Yorkshire) only to be handed over in chains to the Romans by Queen Cartimandua – a betrayal that would eventually provoke an uprising against her rule, led by her own husband.

Old Oswestry Northwest Shropshire

One of a large number of defended enclosures lining the
Welsh borderland in what is now northwest Shropshire,
Old Oswestry presides over a territory that saw minimal
Roman influence until its annexation by Ostorius Scapula
and his four legions in AD 48. Little by way of fine metalwork
or pottery has come to light in the area, which may have
belonged to either the Ordovices or the Cornovii tribes.

The scale of its ramparts suggests this fort was probably
a stronghold of the latter, whose southern borders will have
ensured more contact with the great hillforts of the Wessex
chalklands, with which this fort bears a passing resemblance.

Begun in the Early Iron Age, the defences were
constructed in four phases. Three layers of concentric
ramparts were excavated in succession, followed in the
century before the conquest by two huge encircling banks
rising to 6 metres (20 feet) in places. The standout feature
at Old Oswestry, however, is its convoluted western gateway,
which includes a series of unusual rectangular depressions
separated by ridges. Whether these were livestock pens,
storage pits or obstacles designed to confuse would-be
attackers is unclear, but they form an arresting sight
from the air.

Also clearly discernible from above are the remnants
of an ancient linear earthwork known as 'Wat's Dyke',
believed to have been built in the post-Roman period,
either to mark the limits of Saxon territory, or that of a
long-forgotten Brythonic chiefdom. A section of the dyke
is visible just behind the house in the bottom right corner
of the photograph.

The disturbances within the fort itself mostly date from
World War I, when the site was used for training soldiers
from a nearby army base in trench digging and explosive
setting – exercises that wrought untold damage on its
archaeology. Among the trainees was a young Wilfred Owen,
who was born on the southern outskirts of Oswestry and
who died in northern France on 4 November 1918, a week
before the signing of the Armistice, aged just twenty-five.

Castell Dinas Brân Llangollen, Denbighshire

'Castle of Crows' is the most widely accepted translation of 'Dinas Brân' – a fitting name for this citadel in the sky, high above Llangollen in the Dee Valley. Most of the legends and fragments of history associated with it date from the post-Norman period, in the early thirteenth century, when the Prince of Powys Fadog, Gryffydd Maelor II, erected a formidable castle on the hilltop. But the earthen ramparts below it date from at least thirteen centuries earlier, when this was a stronghold of the Ordovices tribe.

Along with their neighbours the Silures to the east, the Ordovices fiercely resisted Roman rule in the second half of the first century AD, marshalled initially by Caratacus (see p. 248) but continuing the fight long after the ill-fated chief of the Catuvellauni had fled north into Yorkshire and been captured.

Tacitus records how it was the Ordovices' massacre of a Roman cavalry detachment that provoked Agricola to invade the region in the AD 70s – a campaign that resulted in the near annihilation of the tribe. Few settlements in the area recovered from the onslaught and it proved easy pickings for Irish invaders once the legions had left in the late fourth century.

Beyond that, little is known about the Iron Age occupants of this fabulously evocative site in the Welsh mountains, which stands sentinel over the main approach to North Wales from central and southern Britain, via the River Dee.

Echoes of its ancient prominence, however, resound through medieval Welsh literature. Among many tales associated with the site is the encounter between a plucky knight named Pain Peverel and a mace-wielding giant called Gogmagog, who is said to have inhabited the ruins back in the Dark Ages. Peverel had heard that no one dared spend the night on the hilltop for fear of being attacked by the ogre, so he and a gang of friends decided to give it a try. A storm duly erupted, in the course of which Gogmagog appeared and challenged the party. Peverel managed to slay him, and as he was dying the giant told how he had first besieged the castle built by the legendary King Brân to repel him. He also revealed that a golden ox was buried somewhere on the hilltop. Other stories talk of a hidden golden harp and even the Holy Grail itself lying beneath the ruins.

Today, as it would have thousands of years ago, the hilltop offers a superb vantage point over the Berwyn Hills to the west and Clwydian Range to the east – a panorama particularly impressive in winter after a snowfall.

Moel Arthur Clwydian Hills, Flintshire

Forming a great heather-clad wall along the northeast
flank of Wales, the Clwydian Hills line the Denbighshire–
Flintshire border in the far northeast of Wales. In the Late
Iron Age this was the heartland of the Deceangli tribe,
descendants of the Gangani, who are believed to have
migrated from Ireland in previous centuries to settle on
the Llŷn Peninsula and Anglesey.

A chain of six impressive Deceangli forts punctuates
the range, and at 456 metres (1,496 feet) Moel Arthur is the
highest and most spectacular of them, thanks to the massive
twin ramparts enfolding its northern flank. An inward-
turning gateway, edged by earthen banks (visible midway
along the path to the right side of the photograph), leads
to the circular top of the fort, where a walkers' cairn covers
what is thought to have been an Early Bronze Age barrow.
Three copper axes discovered at Moel Arthur after heavy
rain in 1962 lend credence to the idea that this may have
been a ceremonial site in the Chalcolithic period.

No record survives of its fate at the hands of the legions,
but we do know from Tacitus that Deceangli were among
the warriors who resisted Paulinus's attack on Anglesey
in the AD 70s. In 1885, a lead ingot was discovered close
to the banks of the River Dee near Chester inscribed with
Vespasian's name and that of the Deceangli, suggesting
that the tribe had been subjugated and were mining for the
Romans by AD 74, when the ingot was cast.

The stiff climb to Moel Arthur from the car park at
its southern base may be profitably extended to include
Penycloddiau, an even larger hillfort, a couple of miles
further north.

Dinas Dinlle Gwynedd

Coastal erosion is rapidly undermining the foundations of this splendid little hillfort near Caernarfon in North Wales. But when it was built back in the Iron Age, on a mound of naturally formed glacial till heaped up 12,000 years ago by melting ice, the citadel lay more than half a mile from the shoreline, beyond a belt of ancient peat bog recently revealed after a high spring tide.

The rising waters inspired a rescue dig in the summer of 2019, during which archaeologists uncovered the base of a circular structure, 13 metres (43 feet) across with walls 2 metres (6½ feet) thick, believed to have been a Roman watchtower or lighthouse. Finds of pottery, coins and an intaglio (a carved gemstone that would have been worn on a ring) dating from between AD 200 and 300 confirm that the site was occupied at this time, though the origins of the fort are undoubtedly in the Middle to Late Iron Age.

The hills framing this aerial view of Dinas Dinlle are those of the Llŷn Peninsula, from left to right: Bwlch Mawr; the twin peaks of Gyrn Goch and Gyrn Ddu; and to the far right, the three summits of the 'Rivals' ('*Yr Eifl*' in Welsh), crowned by the great hillfort of Tre'r Ceiri (see overleaf).

Between these last two massifs lies the main pass across the Llŷn at Llanaelhaearn, which from the sixth century AD formed an important landmark on the Celtic Christian pilgrimage path to Bardsey Island. Following a chain of early chapels, carved crosses, monasteries, sacred springs and prehistoric stone circles, the route to the 'Island of 20,000 Saints', off the far western tip of the Llŷn, ranked among the most revered in medieval Europe. In the twelfth century, Pope Callixtus II declared the pilgrimage to it the equivalent of one journey to Rome, which greatly boosted its popularity. Today, a specially waymarked path along the coast to Bardsey is popular with long-distance walkers in the summer.

Tre'r Ceiri Llŷn Peninsula, Gwynedd

If one hillfort could be said to epitomize the spirit of Iron Age Wales, it is this eagle's-nest settlement on the Llŷn Peninsula. The site, believed to have been settled by the Gangani tribe that Ptolemy refers to as having originated near the mouth of the River Shannon in Ireland, combines an extraordinary setting with some of the best-preserved hut circles in Europe.

Dubbed in local folklore 'the Hill of Giants', the fort sprawls over a sloping plateau at 485 metres (1,590 feet) encircled by drystone ramparts and spectacular slopes of pale-grey scree. The walls, which were surmounted by a parapet that could be accessed from the interior via ramps at various points, are pierced by three narrow gateways leading to passages that funnelled visitors inside (visible along the top of the fort in the photograph).

The outlines of around 150 huts survive on the summit plateau in an almost miraculous state of preservation. They are mostly circular in plan and would have been roofed in turf and wood, though over time larger huts were subdivided. Towards the end of the period of settlement, a handful of more rectangular structures were added, while a scattering of oval, terraced enclosures and stock pens have also been identified outside the walls, where a spring would have provided a source of fresh water for the four hundred or so people who inhabited this cloud-swept spot.

Most of the finds unearthed at Tre'r Ceiri – including an exquisite gold-plated brooch in La Tène style (now displayed in the Roman Gallery at the National Museum of Wales in St Fagans, Cardiff) – date from the Romano-British period, between AD 100 and 400, though some vestiges date back to 200 BC.

The summit of the hill also holds a large, Early Bronze Age cairn. From on top of it, a sublime view extends northwest over the Menai Strait to Anglesey, west across the Irish Sea to the Wicklow Hills and southwards to the Rhinogs and beyond Cardigan Bay to the carns of distant Pembrokeshire, nosing above the horizon. There are few panoramas like it in Britain, and the sense of space and light you experience here on clear days must have been a tonic after the mist and drizzle that more often prevails at these altitudes on the Llŷn.

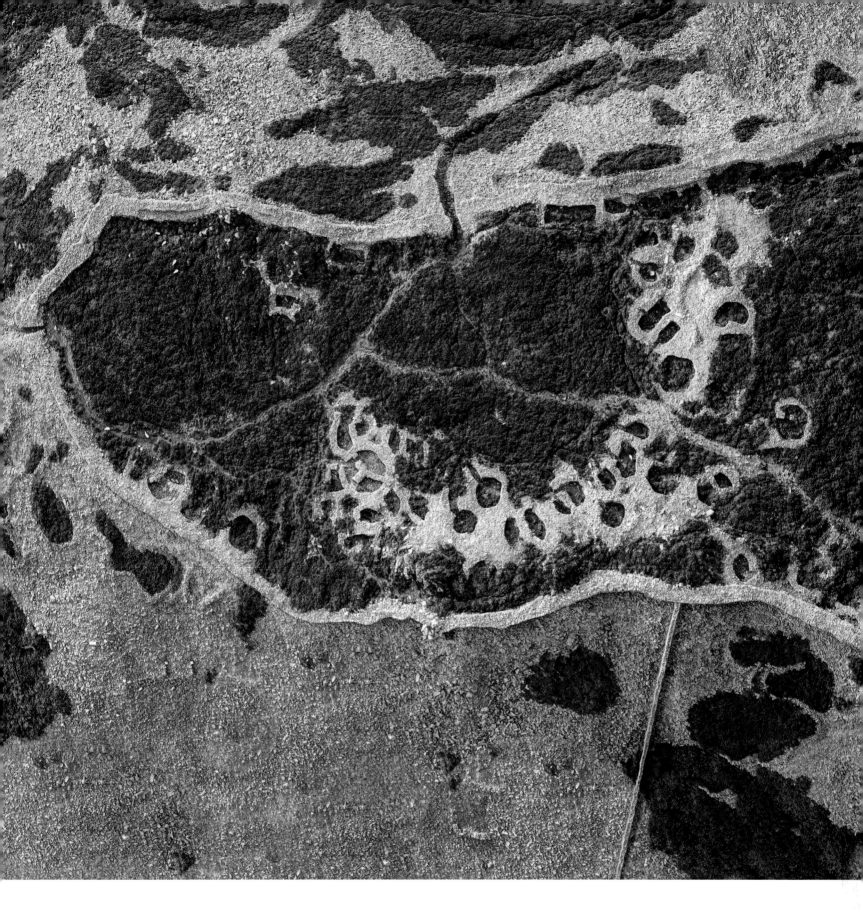

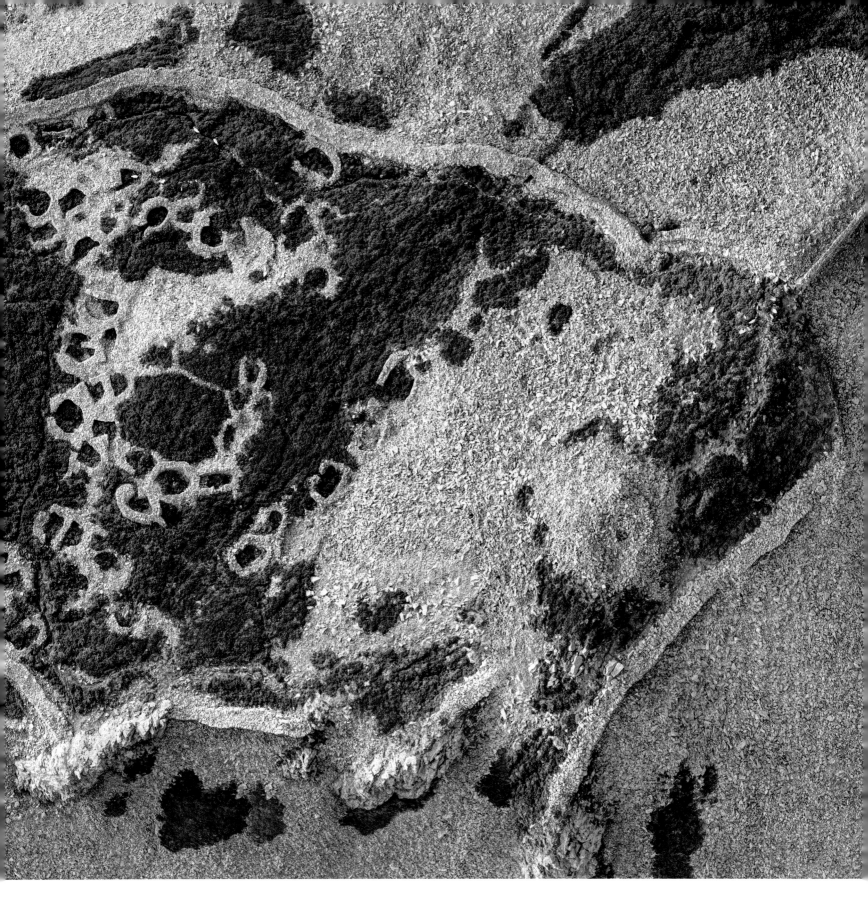

Iron Age Houses

While most of the dwellings that have been reliably dated to the Neolithic period in Britain were roughly rectangular in plan, from the Bronze Age onwards houses tended to be round. Considerable variation occurs across the country, but the basic blueprint, with a conical thatch roof supported by a circle of timber posts, held sway for two and a half thousand years, from the arrival of the Beaker migrants until the arrival of the Romans.

In the Early and Middle Iron Age, roundhouses were modest in size, rarely exceeding 6 metres (20 feet) in diameter. But by the second century BC, average diameters frequently extended over 11 metres (36 feet) and often included a second, inner circle or square of posts to support the rafters.

The inner space was divided between a living area inside the timber pillars, where a hearth was located, and a storage-cum-sleeping area between the outside of the posts and the point where the rafters reached the floor. Sometimes, a low external wall of stone supported the roof beams. Smoke from the central fire would percolate through the thatch, or be channelled out via a gulley.

Bodrifty

Usually, the doorway of Iron Age roundhouses would be orientated towards the winter solstice sunrise in the southeast. Towards the end of the period, porches with internal and external doors to exclude the draughts were also common.

Among numerous regional variations on this basic plan was the 'courtyard house' – common in West Cornwall – where dwellings comprised a cluster of rooms and byres opening on to an enclosed yard. Examples of this type include the settlements of Chysauster and Carn Euny in West Penwith (pictured opposite), both of which date from the early Romano-British period.

Din Lligwy on Anglesey (bottom right) exemplifies how straight lines had begun to be incorporated into British homesteads by the end of the Roman era.

Beautiful, expertly built reconstructions of Iron Age roundhouses may be visited at several sites in the UK, including Butser Ancient Farm in Hampshire, Castell Henllys Hillfort in Pembrokeshire and the National Museum of Wales at St Fagans in Cardiff. At Bodrifty Farm in West Cornwall, it is even possible to spend the night in one.

Holyhead

Holyhead

Holyhead

Chysauster

Chysauster

Carn Euny

Bodrifty

Tre'r Ceiri

Din Lligwy

263

Wittenham Clumps and Dyke Hills South Oxfordshire

The period between Julius Caesar's invasion of Britain in 53 BC and the Claudian invasion of AD 43 was one of great transformation in the southeast of England. Coin evidence shows how the region's various Iron Age tribes settled into distinctive entities at this time and, while dynastic bickering continued, full-scale inter-tribal warfare seems to have given way to long spells of peace and stability. Trade with the Continent flourished, bringing in a range of new luxury goods, notably wine and fancy ceramics associated with its consumption.

Thus, the Thames emerged as Britain's principal trade artery. Hillforts in the southeast were gradually deserted and new types of linear defences constructed to protect lower-lying settlements, known as 'oppida', where mints, courts and markets were situated, often at strategic locations on river banks.

A prime example lies to the south of Dorchester-on-Thames, in the Upper Thames Valley, which had served as a major crossing point for the river in the Early Iron Age, and

probably long before. Settlement in this area had originally been focused on the hillfort of Sinodun (aka 'Castle Hill', one of the wooded tops collectively referred to as 'Wittenham Clumps'), which had been occupied from the Late Bronze Age, around 1000 BC. The photographs on this spread reveal the size and extent of the hillfort's earthen ramparts before the start of the first century BC, when the stronghold was deserted in favour of a site at river level.

Known as 'Dyke Hills', the oppidum ranked among the largest ports in Britain in its day. No archaeology of note has been carried out at the site since Augustus Pitt Rivers' digs of the 1870s, though crop marks in dry summers reveal the outlines of many circular structures and a street plan. These much ploughed and levelled acres have also yielded a higher concentration of Iron Age coins than anywhere else in Britain.

In the photograph overleaf, the massive ramparts that enclosed Dyke Hills on its landward side can be clearly seen, along Castle Hill, the wooded hillock furthest left in the background.

Further Reading

Coming from a background in modern languages, anthropology and South Asian studies, I had to work my way through a lot of books before I felt able to make a start on writing this one. Here is a rundown of those I found most useful.

General Overviews

As an introduction to the subject of British prehistory, Barry Cunliffe's *Britain Begins* (OUP, 2012) is in a class of its own. A well-thumbed copy accompanied me on all my research trips and I still regularly re-read chapters, marvelling at the depth and breadth of Sir Barry's scholarship, and the fluency of his writing. Of particular interest is the way the different periods are related to their wider European context, reminding us that although we may be an island nation, our roots extend far across the Continent in both time and space.

More avuncular and informal in style, Francis Pryor's *Britain BC: Life in Britain and Ireland Before the Romans* (Harper Perennial, 2003) conveys a strong sense of the overall chronology as well as revealing how this knowledge has been pieced together over generations of painstaking work on (and under) the ground.

Mike Parker Pearson's misleadingly titled *Bronze Age Britain* (English Heritage, 2005) is actually the best concise introduction to British prehistory in print, covering the full span from the Mesolithic to the Iron Age, at just the right level of detail if you want to gain a grip on the subject without devoting days to the task, and it's richly illustrated.

Alice Roberts's *Ancestors: A Prehistory of Britain in Seven Burials* (Simon & Schuster, 2022) offers a more personal, experiential read, though one backed up by great insights into the science underpinning modern archaeology. As you'll have gathered from her Foreword to this book, Alice manages to transform subjects that in other hands may come across as bone dry into something meaningful and emotionally engaging, and that's particularly true of *Ancestors*, which is one of the few overviews that could genuinely be described as 'unputdownable'.

Palaeolithic–Mesolithic

My go-to introduction for this sprawling, complex field was Nick Barton's excellent *Ice Age Britain* (English Heritage, 2005), which somehow manages to make sense of all the taxonomies and nomenclature in under 150 pages.

The Neolithic

The World of Stonehenge by Duncan Garrow and Neil Wilkin (British Museum Press, 2022) is a richly illustrated introduction to the period between 4000 and 1000 BC, using the monument as a springboard for explorations of the ways of life that revolved around it.

Julian Thomas's *Understanding the Neolithic* (Routledge, 2004) and Vicki Cummings's *The Neolithic of Britain and Ireland* (Routledge, 2017) both offer solid introductions to the varied types of monuments characterizing the era, and the different ways archaeologists have interpreted them – though both books are pitched more at undergraduates than the general reader.

I found the two-volume *Gathering Time* by Whittle, Healy and Bayliss (Oxbow, 2015) an indispensable source on the archaeology of causewayed enclosures – though again, one primarily for the specialist.

Bronze Age

With essays on subjects as diverse as copper mining, plant cultivation and seafaring, the encyclopaedic *Oxford Handbook of the European Bronze Age* edited by Harry Fokkens and Anthony Harding (OUP, 2013) offers chapter and verse on this pivotal period in prehistory.

British Barrows: A Matter of Life and Death by Ann Woodward (Tempus, 2000) brilliantly decodes Early Bronze Age burial mounds and provides a wealth of tips on where to find the most spectacular examples, while *Ritual in Early Bronze Age Grave Goods* by Ann Woodward and John Hunter (Oxbow, 2015) showcases the extraordinary objects found in them.

Iron Age

Barry's Cunliffe's forensic *The Ancient Celts* (OUP, 2018) covers the many roots and branches of the European Iron Age, situating life in Britain during the first millennium in its broader continental context. His weightier, more detailed *Iron Age Communities in Britain* (Routledge, 2011) sets out a wealth of detail with hundreds of diagrams and maps as well as text. It kept me company during those long, solitary days of the first Covid lockdown in the spring of 2020 and proved revelatory.

Gazetteers

Organized by region, *The Old Stones* by Andy Burnham et al (Watkins, 2018) covers more than a thousand of Britain and Ireland's most noteworthy prehistoric sites, with hundreds of photos, dozens of maps, site plans for the larger locations and fascinating features on subjects such as acoustic theory and celestial alignments. My copy lives in the glove compartment of my van and has led me to many wonderful discoveries.

Wild Ruins BC: The Explorer's Guide to Britain's Ancient Places by Dave Hamilton (Wild Things, 2018) is only marginally less comprehensive, and includes Iron Age hillforts as well as megalithic sites.

On Specific Sites

The Brochs of Gurness and Midhowe by Noel Fojut (Historic Scotland, 2001)

Grime's Graves by Peter Topping (English Heritage, 2011)

How to Build Stonehenge by Mike Pitts (Thames & Hudson, 2022)

Maeshowe and the Heart of Neolithic Orkney by Sally Foster (Historic Scotland, 2015)

Maiden Castle by Niall Sharples (English Heritage, 1991)

Prehistoric Avebury by Aubrey Burl (Yale University Press, 1979)

Stonehenge: Exploring the Greatest Stone Age Mystery by Mike Parker Pearson (Simon & Schuster, 2013)

The Story of Silbury Hill by Jim Leary and David Field (English Heritage, 2010)

Acknowledgments

This book has been a long time in the making and many people have contributed, both directly and indirectly, to its contents, from the Welsh hill farmer who pointed out Moel Goedog after I'd taken a wrong turn above Harlech, to the numerous authors and archaeologists whose books steered me to sites I'd otherwise never have heard of.

First and foremost, I'd like to thank the Commissioning Editor at Thames & Hudson, Philip Watson, for spotting my work on Instagram and recognizing its potential. I don't think either of us knew at the outset what a rollercoaster the project would turn out to be, but I'm grateful he and his colleagues kept the faith through the tempestuous winter of 2021–22. Without Philip's vision and steadying hand, this book would simply not have seen the light of day.

I'm also grateful to designer Maggi Smith, for devising a beautiful layout and making elegant pages from often oddly cropped photographs and text of irregular lengths. Emma Barton did an impressively thorough copy edit in double-quick time. And Celia Falconer and the repro team at T&H were unfailingly patient with my nitpicking notes on colour rendition.

I'm indebted to Kate and Damon Moore for creating the perfect environment in which to research, write and edit my photographs: the Silk Mill studios in Frome proved a true haven in the pandemic and kept me afloat through the tribulations of this book's latter stages.

I'd like to express my gratitude to those friends and colleagues who encouraged me to pursue what felt on many occasions like a madcap venture: Rhiannon Batten, Olivia Clifton-Bligh, Daniel Petkoff and Julia Gibson in particular, gave me confidence in my work when I really didn't have a clue what I was doing, as did a constant stream of positivity from my followers on social media. Thank you to them and to everyone who contributed to my Crowdfunder campaign, especially Stella East, Paul Mulholland, Tim Ager and Janet March. William Dalrymple and Olivia Fraser left some generous comments on Instagram, which spurred me on in the early days, as did the supportive Tweets of Professor Alice Roberts and praise for my images on stage during her 'Ancestors' tour, which brought my photography to the attention of many who would otherwise not have encountered it.

Alice's thoughtful Foreword is one of the highlights of this book and I'm immensely grateful to her – not least for introducing me to Dr Matt Pope, who reviewed the Palaeolithic-Mesolithic chapter, and Richard Osgood, who checked the Iron Age accounts. Dr Penny Bickle and Dr Jodie Lewis reviewed the Neolithic and Bronze Age sections and their comments proved invaluable. Thank you all four of you for your generosity, expertise and encouragement.

My old friend and former publisher Mark Ellingham recklessly agreed to act as my agent after I sent him some of my photographs to look at, and steered this project from pipe dream to the threshold of a publishing deal. Thank you to him for making me feel the project was a worthwhile endeavour, and for devoting so much time and effort to helping to make it happen.

Most of the work for the book was by necessity, and due to having been conducted for the most part during a pandemic, a solitary business. But in the early summer of 2019 I spent a memorable few days staying in the wonderful Iron Age hut at Bodrifty Farm in West Penwith, where Penny and Fred Mustill made me very welcome. Thank you to them, and their daughter Emma, for their hospitality and for making such an atmospheric place to stay in the hills above Penzanze. Find out more about the roundhouse at www.bodrifty.co.uk (or book through www.hiddenhideaways.co.uk).

Last but by no means least, I'd like to thank my two long-suffering sons, Morgan and Aeris, who have lived with this book from its inception, enduring endless marches, frosty dawns and dull lectures on prehistory with fortitude and equanimity. I hope one day you'll share my enthusiasm for those 'mounds' you made me promise never to force you to walk to again, and that they will bring as much joy to you as they have to me. I dedicate this book to you, and to your children, and to theirs …

Sources of Illustrations

All photographs © David R. Abram except:

18: © The British Museum/Trustees of the British Museum

21: © Oxford University Museum of Natural History

22: © The British Museum/Trustees of the British Museum

24: © The British Museum/Trustees of the British Museum

36: Museum of Archaeology and Anthropology, Cambridge. Photo South West Heritage Trust

74: © The British Museum/Trustees of the British Museum

205: © National Museums Scotland

259: © National Museum of Wales

Index Page references in **bold** refer to illustrations.

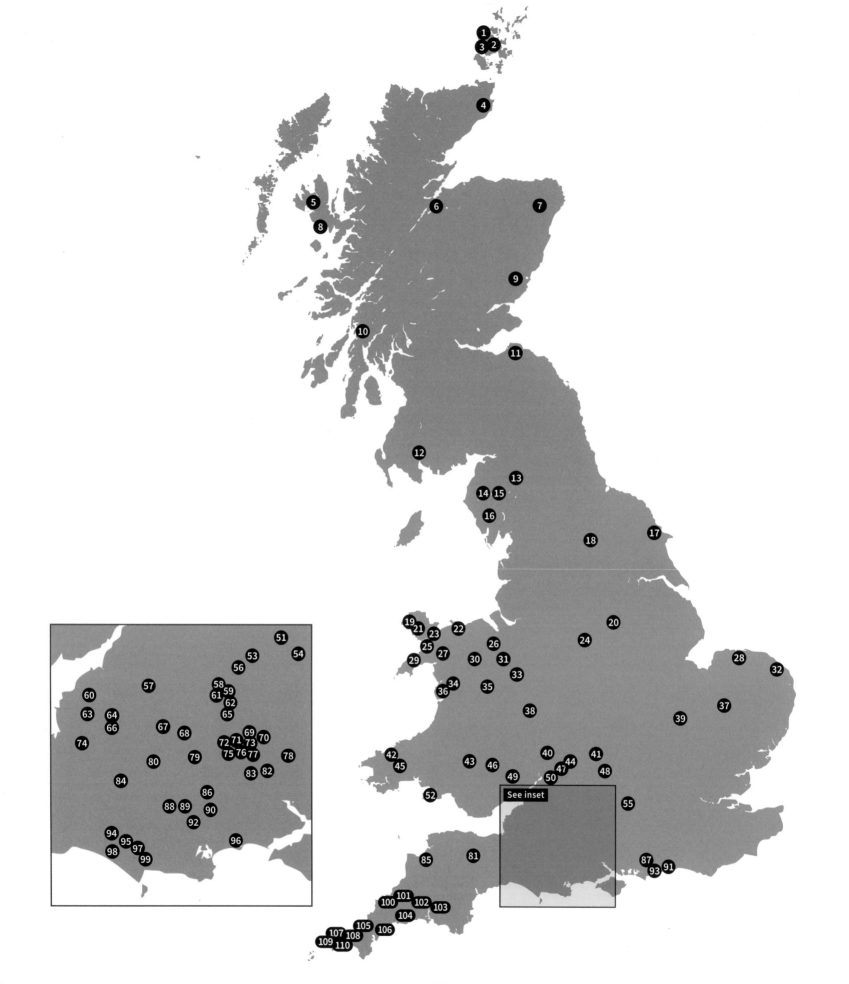